Differentiation Is an *Expectation*

A School Leader's Guide to Building a Culture of Differentiation

Kimberly Kappler Hewitt, PhD
Daniel K. Weckstein

Routledge
Taylor & Francis Group
New York London

First published 2011 by Eye On Education

Published 2013 by Routledge
711 Third Avenue, New York, NY 10017, USA
2 Park Square, Milton Park, Abingdon, Oxon OX14 4RN

Routledge is an imprint of the Taylor & Francis Group, an informa business

Copyright © 2011 Taylor & Francis

All rights reserved. No part of this book may be reprinted or reproduced or utilised in any form or by any electronic, mechanical, or other means, now known or hereafter invented, including photocopying and recording, or in any information storage or retrieval system, without permission in writing from the publishers.

Notices
No responsibility is assumed by the publisher for any injury and/or damage to persons or property as a matter of products liability, negligence or otherwise, or from any use of operation of any methods, products, instructions or ideas contained in the material herein.

Practitioners and researchers must always rely on their own experience and knowledge in evaluating and using any information, methods, compounds, or experiments described herein. In using such information or methods they should be mindful of their own safety and the safety of others, including parties for whom they have a professional responsibility.

Product or corporate names may be trademarks or registered trademarks, and are used only for identification and explanation without intent to infringe.

Library of Congress Cataloging-in-Publication Data

Hewitt, Kimberly Kappler.
Differentiation is an expectation : a school leader's guide to building a culture of differentiation/Kimberly Kappler Hewitt and Daniel K. Weckstein.
    p.   cm.
ISBN 978-1-59667-164-5
1. School improvement programs.
2. Individualized instruction.
3. Active learning.
I. Weckstein, Daniel K.
II. Title.
LB2822.8.H48 2011
371.2'07—dc22   2010033505

ISBN: 978-1-596-67164-5 (pbk)

Also Available from Eye On Education

How the Best Teachers Differentiate Instruction
Elizabeth Breaux and Monique Boutte Magee

Handbook on Differentiated Instruction for Middle and High Schools
Sheryn Spencer Northey

**Differentiating Assessment in Middle and High
School English and Social Studies**
Sheryn Spencer Waterman

**Differentiating Assessment in Middle and High
School Mathematics and Science**
Sheryn Spencer Waterman

Differentiated Assessment for Middle and High School Classrooms
Deborah Blaz

Differentiated Instruction: A Guide for Middle and High School Teachers
Amy Benjamin

**Differentiated Instruction Using Technology:
A Guide for Middle and High School Teachers**
Amy Benjamin

Differentiated Instruction: A Guide for Elementary School Teachers
Amy Benjamin

**Differentiated Instruction for K-8 Math and Science:
Activities and Lesson Plans**
Mary Hamm and Dennis Adams

**Differentiating by Readiness:
Strategies and Lesson Plans for Tiered Instruction Grades K–8**
Joni Turville, Linda Allen, and LeAnn Nickelsen

Differentiating by Student Interest: Strategies & Lesson Plans
Joni Turville

**Differentiating by Student Learning Preferences:
Strategies & Lesson Plans**
Joni Turville

Dedication

To the faculty and staff of Oakwood City School District.
We honor your focus and dedication to
doing what's best for kids.
This book wouldn't exist without you.

Acknowledgments

With gratitude and humility, we thank the following people without whom this book would not be possible:

- Our colleagues Joe Boyle, Gretchen Loper, Nance Bradds, Paul Waller, Allyson Couch, Bruce Saunders, and Mary Jo Scalzo for taking this journey with us and providing anecdotes, examples, and ideas for this book. Your contributions are priceless. We are fortunate to have you as colleagues.
- The exemplary educators of Oakwood whose work we have the honor of showcasing in this book.
- The Oakwood Board of Education for allowing us to share district documents, forms, and artifacts.
- Bob Sickles of Eye On Education for his confidence and support throughout this process—and for his patience in answering our myriad questions.
- Our past colleagues and friends who have helped form who we are as educators and leaders. Specifically, Dan thanks his dad, Don Weckstein, and his former principal at Hopewell Junior School, Dave Pike. Kim thanks Nancy Lyle and John Campbell, her former administrators at McConnell Middle School.
- Our wonderful families for loving us, supporting us, cheering for us, and being patient while we committed our time and energy to this project.

Table of Contents

Meet the Authors ix
Acknowledgments xi

1 Introduction: Why Would You Read This Book? 1
   First Things First: What Is Differentiation? 2
   Who Are We and Why Would You Listen to Us? 3
      How Do We Know Differentiation Is Working for Us? 3
      A Little Bit More about Oakwood 5
      Why We Are Relevant 6
   Can Differentiation Work in a High-Need School or District? 7
   What Can You Expect from This Book? 9
   Research and Data 10

2 Foundations of Change: District, School, and Teacher Goals 13
   Core Values: A Necessity 14
   Goals 18
      District Goals 19
      School Goals 19
      Teacher Goals 22

**3 Change Agents Are Knowledgeable Leaders:
The Value of a Professional Learning Community** 25
   Professional Learning Communities 29
      Walk-Throughs 30
      Artifact Sharing or Critical Friends Session 32
      Book Study and Discussion 35
      Benefits and Byproducts of Our Administrative PLC 37
      Creating Your Own PLC 38

4 Beckoning: "Light" Strategies 41
   Fire and Light Metaphor 41
   Teacher Leadership 42
   Modeling 44
   Professional Development 45
   Celebration 51

5 Pushing: "Fire" Strategies 55
"Fire" Strategies 56
Differentiated Supervision 57
Evaluating Teacher Differentiation and Differentiating Teacher
    Evaluation 61
"Required Choice" Professional Development 73
The Toxic 2 74

6 Assessment, Instruction, Materials, and Technology: Tools to Support Differentiation 77
Assessment: The Linchpin of the Differentiated Classroom 78
    Preassessment 78
    Formative Assessment 90
Differentiated Instructional Approaches 91
    Writing Workshop 91
    Reading Workshop 92
    Inquiry 93
    Math Investigations 94
Instructional Materials Aligned to Differentiation 95
Technology to Support the Differentiated Classroom 96
Differentiated Programming 98

7 Communicate! Communicate! And Then Communicate Some More! 101
Which stakeholders need to be informed? 102
    Teachers 102
    Students 102
    Parents 103
    Administrators 103
    Board of Education 103
What do they need to know? 103
    Teachers 103
    Students 104
    Parents 104
    Administrators 105
    Board of Education 105
What methods will be used to inform them? 106
    Teachers 106
    Students 107
    Parents 111
    Administrators 112
    Board of Education 113

8 Staffing 119
How Do You Hire *the Best*? 120
    Step 1: Sifting through applications and résumés 120
    Step 2: Putting an interview team together 121
    Step 3: Asking interview questions to gain insight into the candidates 122
    Step 4: Discussing each applicant and hiring *the best*! .. 123
    Step 5: Orienting and mentoring the newly hired teachers .. 124
New Teacher Orientation 124
Mentoring the New Teacher 127

9 Jungle to Greenhouse 131
Recognize the Importance of Differentiation 132
Set Goals 133
Learn Together 133
Develop Teacher Leaders 133
Model Differentiation 134
Expect and Push 134
Think Systemically 134
Communicate! 134
Hire *the Best* 135
A Final Thought 135

Meet the Authors

Dr. Kimberly Kappler Hewitt has served since 2005 as director of curriculum, instruction, and assessment for Oakwood City School District in Ohio. Previously, she served as an elementary school principal and district instructional specialist in Norwood, Ohio, an urban Appalachian community near Cincinnati. Prior to that, she taught middle and high school students in Gwinnett County, Georgia. She earned her PhD in educational leadership at Miami University of Ohio and her MEd from Vanderbilt University. She has presented at a number of state and national conferences. Kim currently serves as president of OhioASCD. She has been selected as a 2010 Emerging Leader by ASCD. She was also recognized as a 2001 *Atlanta Journal/Constitution* Georgia Honor Teacher.

Daniel K. Weckstein has served as principal of Oakwood Junior High School since 2007. He served for seven years as assistant principal of Hopewell Junior School in Lakota Local Schools, a very large suburban district near Cincinnati, Ohio. Prior to his service in junior high school administration, Dan taught at the junior high level for five years. In addition to having the opportunity to present at multiple national conferences, Dan was honored as an ASCD Scholar at the 2010 ASCD annual conference. He earned his bachelor's degree from Indiana University and his master's degree from Xavier University. Dan lives in Oakwood with his wife, Kellie, and their children, Collin and Casey.

1

Introduction: Why Would You Read This Book?

> ***This chapter will***
>
> 1. provide a working definition of differentiation
> 2. identify the intended audience for this book
> 3. provide references regarding research about the benefits of differentiation
> 4. introduce readers to our district and share our district data in support of differentiation
> 5. provide an overview of the content of this book

Imagine for a moment . . .

Frank has been teaching high school American history for three decades. He believes that lecture is always best—he can cover more content more efficiently than with other teaching approaches, and it gets kids ready for college, where many of their professors will lecture. When you peer into Frank's classroom, you see student desks in rows facing the whiteboard. Frank stands tall at the front, his notes in front of him, delivering an impassioned lecture on the events leading up to the American Revolution. Some students studiously take notes, others face the teacher, ostensibly listening, while others surreptitiously text friends, stare out the window, or work on the assignment due for their next class.

Tameca is also a veteran American history teacher. She believes that students learn best when they are actively constructing concepts and knowledge. She also values learning activities that are informed by her students' various ways of learning and their readiness levels. As part of the unit on the Revolutionary War, Tameca had her students read one of three selections—of varying Lexile levels and complexity—and capture what they believed to be the key details from their reading on either the graphic organizer that Tameca provided or one of their own creation. When you peer into Tameca's room, you see students working in four different centers. A cluster of students is watching a United Streaming video clip about the events leading up to the American Revolution. Another group is gathered at a table playing MultiMedia Learning's Causes of the American Revolution Game. Still another group is translating the Declaration of Independence into modern-day vernacular. A final group is role-playing a debate between loyalists and patriots. Tameca moves among the groups, monitoring, answering questions, and, when necessary, prodding. Students are variously listening, watching, debating, playing, moving—learning about the causes of the American Revolution in ways that best facilitate their own learning.

Which classroom would you rather learn in? Which teacher would you rather have for your own child? Tameca's room exemplifies the type of learning that takes place in a differentiated classroom. Her class is not about *covering* content but about *learning* content. Her class is not about her preferences as an adult but about how students learn best.

Now imagine a whole school of classrooms like Tameca's. The picture in your head right now is what a school culture of differentiation looks like, and getting there is the purpose of this book. The achievement of that vision will take skillful, tenacious leadership. This book will serve as a guide for leaders who envision such a school. Such leaders include teacher leaders, instructional coaches, professional learning community (PLC) facilitators, principals, curriculum directors, and superintendents. You, as a leader, will determine whether differentiation takes hold and becomes embedded in a school culture of learning or is dismissed as just another passing educational fad.

First Things First: What Is Differentiation?

We borrow our definition from differentiation guru Dr. Carol Ann Tomlinson (1999): Differentiation is "modifying content, process, and/or product according to student interest, readiness, and learning profile."

Content is what is taught, the standards and objectives. *Process* is how it is taught, the instructional approaches, strategies, and activities. *Product* is how students show what they know, which could be through a written test, a presentation, a piece of creative writing, a podcast, or other means.

Student *interest* refers, quite simply, to what interests students, on both a classroom level and individual level. Student *readiness* includes prior and prerequisite knowledge as well as ability. Tomlinson's *learning profile* includes learning style and modality (visual, auditory, tactile), hard-wired brain preferences (e.g., multiple intelligences and Sternberg's analytical, creative, and practical abilities), and gender and culture (Tomlinson, 2010; Sternberg, 1985).

This definition underpins our use of the word *differentiation* throughout this book.

The fact that you are reading this book suggests that you are already committed to change for differentiation. While you might not need to be convinced of the effectiveness of differentiation at improving student learning, some of your stakeholders might. For this reason, we have included at the end of the chapter an overview of recent studies that demonstrate the power of differentiation for improving student achievement.

Who Are We and Why Would You Listen to Us?

We—Kim and Dan, the authors of this book—are administrators in Oakwood City School District near Dayton, Ohio. Our district has been working on differentiation for about ten years now. During the first six we stumbled and failed to maintain focus and momentum toward our goal of making differentiation part of the district's culture. Since 2005, when we renewed and reenvisioned our efforts, we have made significant strides. Thus we are in a position to share what works, as opposed to what we learned the hard way does not work. This book provides a first-person account of carrying out a district-wide change initiative for differentiation. We have lived it and breathed it.

How Do We Know Differentiation Is Working for Us?

Check out our data:

ACT data: Our most recent average American College Test (ACT) composite score of 26.3 (possible scores range from 1 to 36) is the highest in the district's history. Further, our ACT composite average has modestly but consistently increased over the last four years.

Ohio achievement tests: In Ohio, students take state tests annually from grade three through grade eight. In reports received by each district, the district's results are compared to its "similar districts"—those districts that are similar to it demographically. Our most recent data (from 2009) show that on all 18 measures, Oakwood met or—much more frequently—exceeded our similar districts' percentage of students passing the tests *and* percentage of students scoring above proficient. This was the first year in which we attained this feat.

Value added data: Our most recent data show that each building in our district, as well as the district as a whole, achieved "above expected growth" on Ohio's value added metric. Value added measures student growth or progress over time, as opposed to a single point of achievement. In other words, Oakwood students' growth over time is greater than the statistical target.

While we are quite pleased with our data, we must be careful about attributing our students' improvement scores to differentiation alone. We all know that "correlation is not causation" and that there are often multiple factors at play that are difficult to control for in social science research. That said, differentiation has been the only district-wide academic, achievement-oriented goal for the past four years, and it has been the main academic goal for each of our buildings. Thus, while we cannot say beyond a shadow of a doubt that our growth and improvement are due to differentiation, we are confident that differentiation is the main cause.

◆ ◆ ◆ ◆ ◆ ◆ ◆ ◆ ◆

Inside Oakwood

So where did we go wrong with the first leg of our push for differentiation?
Way back in the 1999–2000 school year, the district decided to focus on differentiation, and the then curriculum director—a new position for Oakwood—led the charge. According to her, because both elementary principals were new to the district and she was herself new to the position of curriculum director, it was the "blind leading the blind."

Nonetheless, the plan was to plant the differentiation seed with the elementary schools, to develop the seedlings, then to grow differentiation into the junior and senior high schools.

The district purchased a copy of Tomlinson's groundbreaking book *The Differentiated Classroom: Responding to the Needs of All Learners* (1999). Tomlinson sent an associate to our district to deliver the keynote address at a professional development day. Following this, the curriculum director conducted a 13-week class about differentiation for interested elementary teachers, for which they were able to earn graduate credit through a local university.

About two dozen teachers participated. After the class, the participants were encouraged to do follow-up lesson development and collaboration with colleagues.

The 13-week class was offered again the following year. About another dozen teachers participated. Then things started to unravel. That summer the district shifted its attention and resources to interdisciplinary units. At the junior and senior high schools, the focus was on peer coaching. Then, the following year, the district became embroiled in the math wars. Differentiation—for the most part—got lost in the shuffle.

What did we learn from our initial foray into differentiation?
- Make sure that leaders have sufficient knowledge of the change initiative.
- Focus on just one thing and keep focusing on that one thing until the change has completely taken root and become part of the culture.
- Work tirelessly to keep the tyranny of the urgent from derailing the change initiative.

This book focuses on our efforts from 2005 and beyond, when we renewed and reinvented our differentiation change initiative. Implicit in this work are the lessons learned from the past.

A Little Bit More about Oakwood

Now that we have hopefully wowed you with our data, let us tell you a little more about our district. We are tiny—just under three square miles. We have about 2,100 students, K–12. Almost 98% of our district is residential. We are located adjacent to the city of Dayton, Ohio, and the University of Dayton. We serve a high socioeconomic demographic; the median income in Oakwood is $58,930[1], and 70% of residents have a college degree. About 93% of our students are white, and only 2.9% of our students are economically disadvantaged. About 77% of our teachers hold advanced degrees. We have five schools, including a kindergarten building, two elementaries, one junior high serving grades 7–8, and one high school. We have active, involved, well-educated parents who have high expectations of the district. Additionally, we

---

1. All statistics from this section come from the Ohio Department of Education, www.ode.state.oh.us.

have earned the highest rating from the Ohio Department of Education since the inception of its system for rating districts.

Wait! Please do not discard this book just because we are a high-achieving, suburban district that serves a primarily white, middle-class student population. You might be thinking, "These people are nothing like us. They've got it easy. We can't do what they can."

Why We Are Relevant

We are not going to lie to you: Oakwood is a community that highly values education. Most people who move into this community of primarily older homes and high taxes do so for the school system. We therefore enjoy a great deal of community support—and scrutiny.

Oakwood likes to think of itself as free of and immune from many of the challenges that plague other communities, including crime, generational poverty, drugs, and community disengagement. And while Oakwood is neither free from nor immune to these problems, we recognize that in other districts these challenges require much more attention, time, and energy of school leaders than they require of us in Oakwood. But even if your district does not look like Oakwood, this book may be of value to you. Give us at least the rest of this chapter to convince you.

Before coming to Oakwood, Kim served as an administrator in a high-need district. There was a pervasive sense of urgency, a compelling need to change. That sense of urgency is absent in Oakwood. Change does not come easily here. Often, our success works against us when it comes to change initiatives. We often hear, "Why do we need to change? We're great already!" Successful districts stay successful only if they are oriented toward continuous improvement. We cannot rest on our past success, and we cannot accept the status quo.

One way that we framed our need for differentiation was in terms of the value added measure that Ohio adopted in 2007. With the advent of value added, consistently passing state tests was no longer sufficient. Instead, we had to demonstrate through value added that our students were consistently making progress from year to year. Additionally, the federal mandate to show adequate yearly progress also impelled us to examine how well we serve different subsets of our population, particularly our students with disabilities. Thus, both the state and federal governments require that schools and districts serve *all* students' needs. Differentiation makes that possible.

Oakwood has a long-standing and fiercely defended culture of teacher autonomy. The prevailing sentiment is that as long as students are learning and succeeding, teachers make their own decisions about what to do in their classrooms. In such a culture, the district ship may have a hundred paddlers all pulling it in different directions, leaving the ship wobbly and without forward progress. Getting all the paddlers to commit their efforts to the same strokes is a sizable challenge in Oakwood, but it is imperative if we are to achieve substantive and widespread change.

We have "those kids" too. Whether you are referring to white students, black students, high-ability and gifted students, English language learners, students with disabilities, female students, male students, retained students, high-income or low-income students, motivated students, or underachieving students, we have them too. If you have more diversity in your school, then you have an even more compelling reason for making differentiation part of your school culture.

Good leadership is good leadership. Period. While Oakwood may look different from your district, the methods that a leader must adopt in your district in order to effect change are probably not exceedingly different from the methods we have used in Oakwood. We all must set meaningful, attainable goals, communicate a compelling argument for the change to stakeholders, employ strategies that both attract and press educators toward the change, hire the right people, and make curricular and instructional decisions that support differentiation.

That said, we recognize that the challenges facing leaders in high-need districts trounce those that we face, and we do not wish to negate those challenges. Nonetheless, we believe that the guidance offered in this book can benefit high-need districts as well.

Anyone reading this book will have to adjust and apply the guidance offered to fit your school's or district's needs. Even if our district were similar to yours demographically—and perhaps it is—your district has a distinct and unique culture and situation that requires you to find ways to—well, differentiate what you do as a leader. Just as no two students are alike, no two schools or districts are perfectly alike. How you approach a change initiative will be particular to your context. This book presents a host of strategies that you can make work for your school or district.

Can Differentiation Work in a High-Need School or District?

The Beecher and Sweeny (2008) study cited in the References shows that differentiation can indeed work in a high-need school. Consider also the excerpt below from a conversation with Oakwood High School principal Paul Waller, whose experience spans four different school districts:

> Differentiation is appropriate for diverse districts because it is all best practice and is all research-based. No matter what kind of socioeconomic, diverse setting you're in, differentiation is the right choice.
>
> I've been in districts with one foot in the emergency room, where we're thinking, "What can we do to bring these scores up?" Differentiation is the answer for them. Because it's best practice, maybe differentiation would have more impact in a diverse school—lead to bigger gains for students. It's proactive—it keeps schools from having to initiate other programs, from being reactive. It's been my experience that where there are a lot of discipline issues, there are a lot of kids not getting their needs met. Teachers who differentiate instruction—I've seen them be successful at any setting.
>
> When I was at Princeton High School as a chemistry teacher, I had 60% minority students, I had a blind student, students on IEPs [individualized education plans], lowest SES [socioeconomic status] to highest SES. The only way I could be successful was if I differentiated. I just didn't know to call it that at the time. Now differentiation is the big initiative at Princeton.
>
> Districts should make differentiation the priority. Where they go wrong is not focusing on it enough. Administrators need professional development and need to model differentiation.
>
> In Oakwood, differentiation is teacher-driven. They have ownership and are empowered. That transfers to students and what students expect. Then the parents expect it. Then it becomes part of the culture.

Kim also saw the value of differentiation in a high-need district. Kim previously served as principal of an elementary school in an urban Appalachian district in the Cincinnati, Ohio, area. The community struggled with generational poverty. About two-thirds of the students at the school received free or reduced-price lunches. While many parents in the district cared fiercely for their children and desired most that their children get the best in life and from their education, some parents did not know how to help their children succeed in school. These parents felt uncomfortable just walking into the school building. They had not had a good school experience themselves and did not feel confident helping their children with schoolwork. Some were single parents (or grandparents) raising several children and juggling multiple jobs; many were dealing with financial difficulty, job loss, and health challenges.

Further, a component of urban Appalachian culture is a tension with academic success. Children often feel pressure not to "get above your raisin'." For many students, striving for higher education or increased earning potential seems an implicit indictment of the way in which they have been raised; striving for anything beyond the community standard suggests that life within the community is inferior.

The school itself constantly fought to increase test scores, and there was a pervasive tension throughout the district to improve the district's rating by the state. Some of the teachers in the school were differentiating instruction—even if they did not know to call it that. They recognized that they had students in their classrooms with a host of different needs and that for the students to be successful, the teacher needed to do different things for different students. Some primary teachers were using flexible grouping. A fourth-grade teacher was using choice boards, another fourth-grade teacher found ways to make learning hands-on, and a sixth-grade math teacher used different models of teacher assistance and support, based on student readiness. Those were the classrooms where the best learning was taking place.

Would a goal focused on differentiation be wise or sufficient for such a school? Wise? Yes. Sufficient? No.

As you will see in the next chapter, we strongly argue for selecting a *few* focused goals for a school or district—regardless of whether the district is Oakwood or Kim's former school. Focused attention on a few, impactful goals will yield far better results for students than trying to achieve all the school's needs at once. It may be counterintuitive and difficult to do so, but successful school leaders must limit their goals and absolutely make one of those goals differentiation.

What Can You Expect from This Book?

Chapter 2 focuses on district, school, and teacher goals as the foundations for change. Without focused, directed, and unfailingly tenacious attention to the goal of differentiation, efforts to make differentiation part of the school culture will fall short. We in Oakwood are by no means gurus of goals, but we do know that having too many goals means that none of them gets accomplished and that it is a constant struggle to keep the tyranny of the urgent from stealing our attention away from our differentiation goal.

Chapter 3 argues that knowledgeable leaders are equipped leaders. Leaders must know what differentiation is, what it looks like in the classroom, and how to support it. We share with the reader our administrative professional learning community and how we use walk-throughs, artifact sharing, critical friends protocol, and book study to help us be skillful leaders for change.

Chapters 4 and 5 are companion chapters that introduce Tomlinson's "fire and light" metaphor. Chapter 4 illustrates "light" strategies for drawing educators toward differentiation, and Chapter 5 focuses on "fire" strategies that drive educators toward differentiation change.

Chapter 6 is about assessment, instructional approaches, and materials that promote differentiation. It also includes information about technology to support differentiated instruction.

When leading change for differentiation, leaders must communicate, communicate, and communicate some more. Chapter 7 is packed with strategies for communicating differentiation change to various stakeholder groups.

One of the most—if not *the* most—important responsibilities of leaders is to hire. How can hiring foster change for differentiation? How can leaders use interviews to identify prospective hires who will be committed to and promote change for differentiation? These are questions that Chapter 8 addresses.

The final chapter of the book introduces the reader to our "jungle to greenhouse" metaphor for making schools places where every child thrives. It also answers the question, "When will you stop focusing on differentiation?"

We hope that this book serves as a valuable guide in your journey to embed differentiation into your school culture.

Research and Data

The studies that we discuss here examine the effects of the full model of differentiation on student learning. By "full model" we mean differentiation for student readiness, interest, *and* learning profile. There is also a large body of research about individual aspects of differentiation, including each of the aforementioned topics. For citations of such research, see Carol Ann Tomlinson's presentation slides for the 2010 ASCD annual conference (Tomlinson, 2010) and Differentiation Central's list of articles (www.differentiationcentral.com/articles.html).

Additionally, the studies cited here speak specifically to the effect of differentiation on *student learning*. We recognize that differentiation has other valuable effects, including positive attitudes about learning and stronger self-concept for students (Lou et al., 1996) and more positive attitudes by teachers toward low-income and minority students (Tomlinson, Callahan, & Lelli, 1997).

The most compelling research supporting implementation of the full model of differentiation comes from Tomlinson, Brimijoin, and Narvaez (2008). Data from multiple years showed increases in student achievement at both an elementary school and a high school that served as the focus of study. The elementary school demonstrated increases in student performance on both the state achievement test and a nationally norm-referenced test across content areas and student achievement levels. Further, "results on the New Standards Reference Examinations (NSRE) indicated substantial growth during the first six years of the differentiation initiative" (p. 19) at the high school. Additionally, the high school enjoyed positive post-differentiation effects on college enrollment, Advanced Placement (AP) enrollment, discipline infractions and expulsions, dropout rates, and school climate. It is rare to find reform initiatives that foster gains across content areas for students of all achievement levels, while incidentally increasing AP participation and decreasing dropout rates. This study speaks strongly to the power of differentiation.

A study of an elementary school that implemented both differentiation and enrichment (Beecher & Sweeny, 2008) showed not only improved achievement on state tests in all content areas and proficiency levels, but also a reduction in the achievement gap between economically disadvantaged students and nondisadvantaged students as well as a reduction in the achievement gap between white students and Asian, black, and Latino students.

Tomlinson (2010) cites Rasmussen's (2006) study showing that students at a Chicago high school receiving more differentiated instruction performed better on the ACT English, math, and reading subtests as well as the composite than students who received less differentiation.

A study (Brighton, Hertberg, Moon, Tomlinson, & Callahan, 2005) looked at the degree to which extensive professional development about differentiation at the middle school level affected student achievement, as well as other factors, such as teacher attitudes. The study compared the treatment group receiving extensive professional development about differentiated instruction and assessment with a treatment group receiving only professional development about differentiated assessment and a control group. Where statistically significant differences in student learning occurred, the differentiation schools invariably showed greater gains in student achievement. Lest the reader be overly impressed, the data suggest that other factors played a role in the differences in student achievement, and the treatment (professional development about differentiated instruction and assessment) had only minor effects on student learning.

References

Beecher, M. & Sweeny, S. (2008). Closing the achievement gap with curriculum enrichment and differentiation: One school's story. *Journal of Advanced Academics*, 19(3), 502–530.

Brighton, X., Hertberg, H., Moon, T., Tomlinson, C., & Callahan, C. (2005). *The feasibility of high-end learning in a diverse middle school.* Research Monograph RM05210. Charlottesville, VA: National Research Center on the Gifted and Talented.

Lou, Y., Abrami, P., Spence, J., Poulsen, C., Chambers, B., & d'Apollonia, S. (1996). Within-class grouping: A meta-analysis. *Review of Education Research*, 66, 423–428.

Rasmussen, F. (2006). *Differentiated instruction as a means for improving achievement as measured by the American College Testing (ACT).* Doctoral dissertation, Loyola University of Chicago School of Education.

Sternberg, R. (1985). *Beyond IQ: A triarchic theory of human intelligence.* New York: Cambridge University Press.

Tomlinson, C. (1999). *The differentiated classroom: Responding to the needs of all learners.* Alexandria, VA: ASCD.

Tomlinson, C. (2010). The demographics, research, and ethics of differentiated instruction. ASCD Annual Conference, San Antonio, TX, March 6.

Tomlinson, C., Brimijoin, K., & Narvaez, L. (2008). *The differentiated school: Making revolutionary changes in teaching and learning.* Alexandria, VA: ASCD.

Tomlinson, C., Callahan, C., & Lelli, K. (1997). Challenging expectations: Case studies of high-potential, culturally diverse young children. *Gifted Child Quarterly*, 41(2), 5–17.

2

Foundations of Change: District, School, and Teacher Goals

> ***This chapter will***
>
> 1. illustrate the necessity of identifying core values and how our district worked through that process
> 2. illustrate the importance of establishing organizational goals in order to achieve success with systemic change
> 3. provide answers and details about the development of school and teacher goals

The bonus in this chapter is that these concepts can apply to any new or ongoing initiative you may be working on in your district. Our focus will, of course, be on differentiation. At times, however, we will generalize to apply to any initiative.

> Vision without action is merely dreaming.
> Action without vision just passes time.
> Vision with action can change the world.
> —Joel Barker

Building a culture of differentiation in our district did not happen just because we said we wanted it to happen. In fact, successfully pushing through new initiatives of any kind does not just *happen*. To be successful, the change must be systemic—with the entire organization moving forward in the same direction.

Core Values: A Necessity

In the 1999–2000 school year, our district originally created a goal centering around differentiated instruction. As described in Chapter 1's *Inside Oakwood*, we had what we thought was a pretty good plan: to start in the elementary schools and eventually move to the junior high and high school.

Unfortunately, after a couple of years, this goal fell by the wayside. It was still in print as a part of our district goals, but other initiatives took its place. As so many districts do, we were trying to do too many things at the same time. We were not making focused, systemic progress toward accomplishing *any* of our goals.

In 2005, our district had a transition of leadership—a new director of curriculum, instruction, and assessment, who had reignited the focus on differentiation, and a new superintendent, who knew the importance of establishing a set of core values tied directly to our vision and mission.

The concept of our district's core values came as a result of a book study led by our new superintendent in 2005. *Transforming Schools: Creating a Culture of Continuous Improvement*, by Zmuda, Kuklis, and Kline (2004), was the focus of our study. The authors referred to two types of systems—incompetent and competent. The practices in an incompetent system stem from assumptions based on perceived reality, having little to no connection to that system's core beliefs. On the other hand, competent systems use systemic thinking that is based on reality—the "brutal facts," as Jim Collins (2001) would put it. To have a competent system, our practices needed to be based on reality and directly linked to our core beliefs.

The process of establishing our core values was so valuable to our district that it is shared here:

♦ ♦ ♦ ♦ ♦ ♦ ♦ ♦ ♦

Inside Oakwood

In May 2005, the superintendent met with district administrators and the Board of Education to discuss our strengths, weaknesses, and the future. Her intention was to bring all of us together to work on a common purpose: identifying our core beliefs. We also discussed how to involve our stakeholders in this process. This experience turned out to be as much a bonding experience as a plan for the future.

Beginning in January 2006, our superintendent hosted 10 focus groups with the purpose of talking specifically about what our district's core values were. Approximately 150 people joined these focus groups—teachers, administrators, students, and community members. Prior to the meeting, all attendees received a worksheet (see Figure 2.1) that gave them advance opportunity to prepare their thoughts for the upcoming discussion.

The results, collated after all the focus groups met, identified recurring themes for each discussion question. Two follow-up sessions were held for those participants who wanted to be our check and balance, ask any follow-up questions, and quench their need for further discussion. These two sessions were quite helpful in facilitating the necessary buy-in from our stakeholders.

The superintendent took all the collated data and narrative details with her to a district administrative team retreat. It was at that off-campus retreat that we began to see our core values, mission, and vision take form. After that retreat, we, as an administrative team, continued drafting, and drafting, and drafting, until we got to the final version (see Figure 2.2) that is still in use today.

This process was not as easy as it sounds here. One of the most frustrating pieces, from the superintendent's point of view, was to work with the administrative team and Board of Education: "It was like pulling teeth to lead them through this process." It was painful for some because they were engaged in something they just could not see translating into practicality. This made it painful for the superintendent because she was receiving the message *Why don't you just put this thing together and we'll make it work?* This difficulty illustrates why persistence is imperative.

♦ ♦ ♦ ♦ ♦ ♦ ♦ ♦ ♦

So we had identified, developed, and adopted our core values—now what? From that point forward, we have worked to link everything we do back to our core values. We make a conscious effort to link district goals, school goals, and teacher goals back to our core values, vision, and mission.

Hopefully you noticed the first line of our mission in Figure 2.2: "Doing what is best for students . . ." This simple, common-sense mission statement has been immensely powerful for our district; it reorients us away from doing what is most comfortable for adults. When our focus is on doing what is best for our kids, it is surprising how many things we see and do differently. As new teachers, administrators, and families enter our district, this statement is one of the first things they talk about. Shouldn't every school be working toward that mission?

What does it take to make this happen? Having someone to champion the core values at every level, in every school, and in every department is

FIGURE 2.1 Core Values Worksheet

Guiding Principles

Please complete the following statements.

Essential elements of an excellent school system are:

The Oakwood School District should be widely known as:

All students in the Oakwood district should have equal opportunity to:

Community involvement in the schools should be:

Efficient use of public resources should:

Graduates of Oakwood High School should:

The attributes that should characterize the Oakwood Schools are:

Reflection Questions

What are the strengths of our school system?

What attributes of the Oakwood Schools are essential to preserve?

What do you think are the most pressing challenges facing the Oakwood Schools?

What do you think are our greatest assets, both inside and outside the schools, for dealing with the challenges we face?

FIGURE 2.2 Statement of Vision, Mission, and Core Values

Oakwood City School District
academic excellence since 1908

Vision

The Oakwood School community educates students to become ethical decision-makers who achieve their life goals, take responsible risks, and contribute to the greater good of the world. Graduates are prepared for their post-secondary pursuits, proud of their Oakwood education, and poised to lead and serve.

Mission

Doing what is best for students is our guiding principle. To this end, the Oakwood School community commits the resources, support, expertise, and experiences needed for all students to achieve.

Core Values

EXCELLENCE: Excellence is our commitment to superior standards in all that we do. We pursue continued growth and strive to achieve the highest levels of performance in all endeavors.

COMMUNITY: Community describes a commitment to our students that is shared by our citizens, families, faculty and staff. Our students thrive when relationships and a sense of common purpose are focused toward making a positive difference in their lives.

TRUST: Trust is the confidence we place in one another to act with integrity and in the best interests of our students.

RESPECT: It is important that we seek ways to demonstrate our understanding of and appreciation for differences among us. All of our students deserve to experience the excellence Oakwood offers in ways that complement their individual strengths and needs.

ACCOUNTABILITY: Accountability is the commitment to examine all endeavors with a constructive and critical eye in order to take responsible and dynamic action.

SERVICE: Going beyond self and giving back to the broader community are essential experiences for personal growth.

TRADITION: We celebrate our history by appreciating our traditions. A shared sense of belonging to a special place inspires commitment to quality.

FUTURE: We honor our history by embracing the future. This requires leadership at all levels that is forward thinking and informed by divergent perspectives.

paramount. The superintendent plays a key role in this process, but so does *every* member of the administrative team. To establish and maintain a successful organization and a competent system, we rely on every member of the team to be on board. This type of distributed leadership protects the district from a loss of direction should the superintendent or other key leader leave. Looking at the big picture involves stepping away from the day-to-day operations and focusing on being a district-wide instructional leader.

In our district since 2005, we have had a change of personnel in five of our nine administrative positions. Sustaining a leadership vision is a significant issue when these changes occur—and they happen in all districts. This is why the core values are essential, and worth the pain of the process. They may take on different emphasis with different people, but our district's values, vision, and mission have remained constant throughout the transitions we have faced. In fact, these values have attracted quality candidates to our district. It is no coincidence that the past two principals we have hired referred directly to the mission statement during the interview process, recognizing that it reflects why we are all here. The core values remain core values no matter who is here, no matter what the economic situation may be, no matter how the district's demographics change, no matter what we are faced with.

Goals

Before going into detail about Oakwood's district, school, and teacher goals, we feel strongly that we must point out that we certainly do not see ourselves as exemplars in goal writing. However, Oakwood is extremely oriented and focused on its differentiation goal. It is this focus and dedication that have held the door open for progress in the district.

A common pitfall in any organization is working on too many initiatives at the same time. This can drive all levels of the organization into the ground, especially the teachers who are pushed in too many directions.

In our district, the concept of differentiation has been an initiative from year to year for more than a decade. Since 2005, however, we have made great strides in differentiation *because we have made differentiation our priority*. Those strides and the strategies and steps behind them are the focus of this book. We made a determined, intentional, and conscious decision that differentiation would be our main focus and that everything else would revolve around that focus. We decided that we were going to be about differentiation in our district. *That is how change can be enacted*. In *Transforming Schools*, Zmuda, Kuklis, and Kline refer to habitual practice rooted in reality (2004); you make the decision, and then you practice it, and practice it, and practice it. That is how competent systems are created, no matter what transitions the district faces.

District Goals

Our district goals are currently developed by looking at the realities that face our district. For example, if we have a levy in the near future, passing that levy will certainly be a goal. These big-picture goals will develop momentum and support in a plan of action (which includes tasks, person responsible for each task, and timeline for completion). The power of each goal is inherent in the action plan. The action plan for any goal must contain detailed, thoughtful, and specific steps that will lead straight toward accomplishment of the goal.

At the district level, each goal may have several subgoals, or clusters coming off the main goal. For example, if passing a levy is a main goal, a subgoal might be earning community recognition for being financially responsible. And once again, the power of that goal will be in the developed action plan.

Although our superintendent is the official author of our district goals, many people play a role in their development. Possible topics and discussions for goals emerge from discussions at cabinet meetings (our monthly or twice monthly administrative team meetings). During those meetings, we discuss not only topics that may evolve into goals, but also how we can and will carry out these goals. Each building is expected to have school goals that tie into district goals. The building principal is expected to tailor the umbrella of the district goals to meet the needs of the school.

As clearly mentioned earlier, all goals—one-year or long-term—are linked to our core values. For example, our district goal of differentiated instruction is linked to our core value of *excellence* and is tied directly to our vision and mission. This goal has been a constant since 2005 and will remain as a district goal for many, many more years. Our goal of differentiation may evolve and look different from one year to the next, but will still revolve around differentiated instruction and will still be linked directly to our core values. And it will continue to be carried out as a goal at the building level, where it will also continue to be a goal in each teacher's classroom.

School Goals

The building principal's role is to take the district goals and magically turn them into school goals that are meaningful and valuable to the school community. Of course, some of the school goals may not tie directly into district goals. However, all school goals must tie into the core values. These are not values for the top level alone; they are core values for every part of the organization.

As building level administrators, we must establish a sense of urgency for these goals; we must be able to sell the importance and necessity of these goals to our staff. If we do this job well, the details of these goals become a *roadmap* for our teachers to drive the concepts into their classrooms. School goals serve as vital links from the district goals to the teacher goals. Development and writing of these goals, and what is done with these goals after writing them, are tasks not to be taken lightly.

This section will include a variety of methods and styles in response to commonly asked questions regarding school goals. Many of the responses below have been successful, but some have not (and that may vary from year to year). Of course, other methods will work too; the main idea is that these questions are considered and acted upon using an approach that will be best for your building.

What role should data play when developing school goals?

All types of data should inform school goals—attendance data, achievement and testing data (ACT, SAT, AP, PSAT, PLAN, state tests, national norm-referenced tests, Adequate Yearly Progress, etc.), graduation and college admission data, and discipline data. These data should be used to identify areas for growth. These areas should be the focus of school and district goals.

While we advocate for *measurable* goals, we caution that overemphasis on writing goals that are quantitatively measurable often leads to writing goals that are artificial, trivial, and unrelated to our overarching purpose of doing what's best for kids.

Who should be involved in the development of school goals?

Undeniably, teachers need to be involved. Even within our small district, however, our building principals greatly vary in their methods here. One principal develops the school goals without much assistance, then asks the staff for feedback and makes any necessary adjustments based on their input. Another principal develops the school goals collaboratively with a leadership team of seven teachers. Those seven teachers are connected to the staff in a variety of ways, so they bring input from the staff to the meetings. Yet another principal uses the previous method a bit differently by handpicking teachers to take on this task. One of these chosen teachers may be typically resistant of anything new because participation in the process compels commitment to the product. Another teacher may be reluctant to give input, but ends up being a very valuable member of the team because it is more awkward to stay quiet than it is to participate in a small group of colleagues.

Whatever the method, the consistent piece is that teachers are involved in one way or another. The initial level of teacher involvement will inversely correlate to the amount of later work that is necessary to get ownership and buy-in from the building staff.

What are the best ways to get buy-in from the staff?
The response to this question is twofold.

1. As just mentioned, the more the school staff is involved in the process of the development of the goals, the more ownership they will have in the product. While the method for involvement differs from building to building, what does not vary is that we offer the opportunity to provide input, feedback, and suggestions. It seems that the more we involve our teachers in this process, the more they accept the goals as their own.
2. Blood, sweat, and tears (well . . . hopefully not any blood). After years of prioritizing differentiation, our teachers realize there is *need* for differentiated instruction. They realize this is a nonnegotiable priority in our district, and they have become our own champions of differentiated instruction. According to Doug Reeves (2009, p. 44), "most people must engage in a behavior before they accept that it is beneficial; then they see the results, and then they believe that it is the right thing to do." This is why we have "fire" strategies to compel change, as discussed in Chapter 5.

The more educated we as a staff became about differentiation, the more we embraced it. We encouraged and pushed a healthy amount of professional development focused on differentiation on our teachers. We empowered teachers to develop professional learning communities centered on differentiated instruction. We brought in respected speakers and sent teams of teachers across the country to attend conferences. Eventually these attempts went in a full circle: our teachers began sharing best practices during staff meetings and in informal conversations in the hallway. They had bought in—they had embraced the goal.

What purpose do school goals serve?
Our school goals should drive everything that we do in the building. School goals provide direction for *all* staff members—teachers, instructional aides, counselors, secretaries, cafeteria staff, administrators. Our school goals provide a reference guide for keeping our focus in line. Our school goals are also an excellent springboard for our teachers to write their own goals, which will be discussed in the next section.

To be frank, this is not always the case in every building or in any building. Often written goals collect dust on a bookshelf. We therefore want to emphasize what purposes school goals should *not* serve:

- School goals should *not* be written to keep the superintendent happy. Just because written goals are required from above, that should not be the driving reason to develop them.
- School goals should *not* be so focused on being measurable and data-based that they become meaningless to the ultimate mission—doing what is best for students.
- School goals should *not* be shared once with the staff and then placed in a file until the end of the year. These goals should be referred to and discussed throughout the year.
- School goals should *not* be the principal's individual goals. Although these are also important, a school needs building-wide goals for guidance through the year.

How are school goals evaluated?

Each principal in our district evaluates the school goals somewhat differently with staff—individually, with a select group of teachers, or with the entire staff. The methods vary just as the process for development varies. One method that is consistent is that we must present the results of our school goals to the administrative team and the Board of Education. At those meetings we share what we did or did not do and how we might do it better. We also share how our goals might evolve in future school years.

Teacher Goals

Teacher goals are specific to what happens in the classroom. This is where the rubber hits the road—this is where differentiation comes alive.

All our teachers are required to write goals for each school year. At least one of their goals *must* have to do with differentiation. The district administrators felt strongly that we should do more than encourage and cajole and recommend; we felt that it is unacceptable for teachers to *opt out* of differentiation. If the district really believed that differentiating instruction is important for student learning, than it should be expected of *all* educators. That was the philosophy behind the differentiation goal requirement. This approach and the concept of teacher goals are more thoroughly discussed in Chapter 5.

In the first weeks of school each year, the building administrator confers with each teacher to discuss the teacher's goals for that school year. Toward the end of the year, the teacher and administrator meet again so the teacher can present evidence of reaching or making progress toward those goals. This process is a part of each teacher's evaluation for the school year.

As administrators, we need to be certain that when the rubber does hit the road, the car is moving in the right direction. For a few teachers, we need to be certain that the tires are actually landing on the road and not the sidewalk. And for others, we need to get out of the road and let them drive.

Our teachers have improved at writing their goals over the years. With time and familiarity, the goals have become much less rigid and much more related to teachers' individual strengths and weaknesses. Their goals have become more specific to what will help their students in the classroom. The teachers seem to have a clearer sense of what they want to work on, and they work to build those thoughts from the framework of the school goals. Getting to this point, however, has taken time and a focus of building a culture for doing what is best for the students in the building.

Summary

District goals, school goals, and teacher goals must all be linked back to the district's core values. These core values will remain our constant in this environment of continual challenge.

The relationship among district, school, and teacher goals is somewhat analogous to how teachers differentiate in the classroom. All classroom teachers are expected to teach the standards to all students. That is nonnegotiable. However, how those standards are taught, how they are extended, and how they are scaffolded and supported are differentiated to meet the needs of the students in the classroom. Similarly, school and teacher goals should reflect district initiatives and commitments. That is nonnegotiable. However, they should be differentiated based on the needs of the individual building and teacher.

References

Collins, J. (2001). *From good to great: Why some companies make the leap and others don't.* New York: Harper Business.

Reeves, D. (2009). *Leading change in your school: How to conquer myths, build commitment, and get results.* Alexandria, VA: ASCD.

Zmuda, A., Kuklis, R., & Kline, E. (2004). *Transforming schools: Creating a culture of continuous improvement.* Alexandria, VA: ASCD.

3

Change Agents Are Knowledgeable Leaders: The Value of a Professional Learning Community

> ***This chapter will***
>
> 1. illustrate the importance of leaders who are knowledgeable about what differentiation is, what research supports it, and what it does (and does not) look like in the classroom
> 2. promote the use of the professional learning community (PLC) model for increasing leaders' knowledge of differentiation and their preparation to lead for differentiation
> 3. provide advice for those who want to create their own PLC

"What about Bob?"

This account comes from Joe, Oakwood's former high school principal:

In the spring of 2006, at a time when Oakwood High School was just beginning to attempt to "sell" the concept of differentiation, I met with a teacher regarding academic concerns we had for Bob. Bob is the sort of student who truly struggles at Oakwood High School. With an IQ of around 85, Bob did not qualify for any special education services. However, in a school such as Oakwood, where 97–98% of the graduates attend college after graduation, Bob—and students like Bob—struggles. Since only three or four students in each grade are not going to college and since the majority of these receive varying levels of special education services, the lower level (i.e., not AP track) core courses are very college preparatory. No core courses are geared for the non-college-bound. The demand just isn't there.

Bob failed Math I as a freshman. During his sophomore year, Bob again struggled along in Math I as he did in all his classes, despite literally hundreds of hours of free tutorial assistance from both a number of his teachers and a very sympathetic guidance counselor. Bob tried. However, Bob had learned long ago that "school did not like him." School was a place of disappointment for Bob. He got the message that he was "dumb," and it took all the inner strength he could muster each day just to get up and enter that "place of failure" again.

Bob's math teacher is known to be a hardworking, well-prepared person. He takes pride in the fact that he is available almost every day for forty-five minutes before school and, when arranged, at lunchtime or after school to tutor students who need help in math. In fact, the teacher expects struggling students to come to him for help during these times. So, when we met to discuss Bob's math grade, which was just below a D, the teacher's first suggestion was that Bob come to his room before classes begin to get tutorial assistance. The teacher pointed out that Bob had pretty much stopped coming for help and that his effort on homework had been, at best, waning.

At first blush this teacher's suggestion seemed both logical and generous. He was willing to tutor Bob in order to help him master the material. Why, then, was I disappointed with the teacher's first and, really, only proposal?

The reason is that the offer to tutor Bob was, to me, a clear indication that this proposed solution was about what the teacher would do and not about what the learner, Bob, needed. To ask Bob to get up an hour before his classmates so that he could experience an extra session of "school doesn't like me" or "I'm stupid" was not an appropriate solution by itself. The teacher needed to do something different for Bob. Bob needed exposure to alternative ways to learn the math, but the teacher's suggestion that Bob come early for tutoring was just more of the same. The teacher was changing nothing and felt Bob just needed to work harder.

That thirty-minute meeting hit me right between the eyes. Here was a hardworking, respected, dedicated teacher who—in my mind—had missed the point. The point is that what we do is about student learning. We are responsible to find ways for our students, whether they be the class valedictorian or Bob, whether they be off to the world of work or off to Yale, to master the core of our content. That is why telling Bob to strive even more is not an acceptable solution. We need to become masters of our own profession who seamlessly adjust our pedagogy (process), our assessment mechanisms (product), and our core material that must be learned (content) so that all the Bobs of the world have the opportunity to be successful.

This does not mean compromising our expectations insofar as passing a course is concerned. Bob must still do a lot of hard work. But it does mean that Bob will be provided the legitimate opportunity to be successful.

One thing became abundantly clear from this meeting: As the educational leader of Oakwood High School, I had a lot of work to do regarding getting our staff to truly understand, embrace, and seamlessly implement differentiation.

We intentionally left this vignette unresolved here because the point is to show that as leaders we need to be able to frame our conversations with the language of differentiation. We want to be able to articulate what differentiation is, why it's critical, and what it looks like. We want to be able to offer strategies and resources to support teachers. We want to be able to explain to parents what we do and why we do it. And we want to be prepared and confident to respond to comments like these:

Teacher: "I'm already doing this differentiation stuff."

We found two types of teachers in this category. The first type was the teachers who were actually doing differentiation in the classroom. We hoped to help these teachers continue to grow in the use of differentiation and also serve as teacher leaders among the staff. Many of these teachers themselves went on to be facilitators of professional learning communities (which are discussed later in this chapter). The second type included teachers who thought they were differentiating, but in reality were not. This brought on another challenge of helping these teachers understand the true meaning of differentiation.

Teacher: "Differentiation is just another fad. It, too, will pass. I don't need to change. I just need to wait it out."

Those of us who have been in education long enough know that some things—like open classrooms—come and go like fads. Other things—like formative assessment for learning—endure. It's important to communicate that differentiation falls in the latter category: it's a sound instructional approach that we will not abandon.

In Oakwood we had several of those reluctant teachers that Phillip Schlechty writes about in his article "On the Frontier of School Reform with Trailblazers, Pioneers, and Settlers" (1993). Characterizing them as "settlers" and "stay-at-homes," he writes, "Settlers need to know what it is they are expected to do and where they are going to go. They need much more detail and more carefully drawn maps than do those who have gone before them. They need to be persuaded that the venture upon which they are being asked to embark is worthwhile." We felt that, as an administrative team, we would be much more able to provide those details and maps if we could articulate what differentiation looked like in a variety of classrooms. We also learned that stay-at-homes refuse to budge and need to be treated with "benign neglect."

Teacher: "If I try tiered assessments, that's going to change how I grade. Am I going to be supported by the principal if a parent questions my new assessment practices?"

We realized that we need to provide freedom to teachers to use different strategies in the classroom, and we need teachers to know that we will defend and support them as they try new strategies and assessment practices. As we administrators learned more about differentiation, we were able to communicate permission to the teachers to take risks with differentiation and experiment to see what works best. We sometimes found teachers reluctant to change their expectations for their students, fearing they would be accused of lowering their expectations. A teacher can still have high expectations for a student, but they might not be the same as the expectations for a student sitting across the room.

Parent: "My child isn't being challenged enough." Or "Why does my child have a different spelling list (or more challenging reading assignment) than other kids?"

Our knowledge gave us the foundation upon which to respond to parents' concerns. We try to communicate to parents that we strive as educators to challenge every child; students may have different work (replacement work), but they shouldn't have more of the same work. We now share a common definition of differentiation and vocabulary to explain what is happening in the classroom. Some forms of differentiation are not obvious to students, let alone to parents. We can explain that parents might not always realize how the teacher is differentiating for a child and that it's a fair question to ask a teacher. Our teachers, similarly, have grown very adept (far more adept than we) at providing examples of the differentiation that they do in their classroom.

In order to be prepared to lead and support differentiation and to address situations like the aforementioned, we need to be sufficiently knowledgeable about differentiation. The next section of this chapter describes how we, as an administrative team, participate in a professional learning community to increase our own knowledge of differentiation and support each other. We strongly recommend that any school or district leaders who are undertaking the role of change agent for differentiation grow their knowledge of differentiation as part of a group of like-minded educators. Going it alone is difficult and isolating. Learning with peers who are similarly engaged in the journey of enculturating differentiation provides crucial emotional and intellectual support from people who will commiserate with the challenges and obstacles that administrators will invariably face.

Professional Learning Communities

The term *professional learning community* (PLC) describes a collegial group of educators who are united in their commitment to student learning and who meet regularly to learn about and focus on a topic. Research (SEDL, 1997) shows that the benefits of PLCs for the staff and students include reduced isolation of educators, increased collegiality, better-informed and committed teachers, and academic gains for students.

In 2006, PLCs were introduced in our district as an optional way for teachers to increase their knowledge of and comfort with differentiation by joining a supportive network of peers. As leaders, we recognized that in forming our own PLC composed of administrators we could model what we hoped the teachers would do and increase our own understanding of differentiation—while supporting each other in this journey.

Professional learning communities mean different things to different people. Our district offers a variety of PLCs to educators each year, and participation in a PLC is optional. Each of our PLCs is focused on some aspect of differentiation, but each differs in its specific focus, the core text that it uses, when and where it meets, its target audience (primary teachers, math teachers, teachers new to differentiation, K–12 teachers generally, etc.), and how it structures its meetings. Our PLCs are facilitated by teacher leaders—but not differentiation gurus—who agree to do the following:

- guide the PLC through its study of the topic
- establish and keep regular schedules
- establish group norms (e.g., how to structure the group's time together, sharing, etc.)
- help to develop the action plan (what the group aims to accomplish)
- establish an emotionally and intellectually safe environment in which people will feel comfortable
- encourage active participation and provide equal opportunity for all voices to be heard
- decide the structure of the group:
  - who will attend (e.g., fifth- through eighth-grade teachers)
  - when the group will meet (e.g., after school on the first Wednesday of each month)

- where the group will meet (e.g., at a local restaurant, through Moodle, at school)
- what text the group will use (e.g., book, videos, podcast, articles, etc.)
- what incentives the participants will receive (e.g., gift cards to a bookstore, instructional materials, food at the meetings)

We have found our own administrative PLC to be so effective and important that we take a good deal of space in the next several pages to describe it. We also provide suggestions for starting one yourself.

Our administrative PLC meets monthly for two hours. We rotate locations; each month we meet in a different building in our district, and the principal of that building is responsible for providing refreshments (we have our priorities!). Our PLC meetings have three key components: walk-throughs, artifact sharing or Critical Friends session, and book study and discussion.

Walk-Throughs

Walk-throughs are unannounced, nonevaluative, five-minute classroom observations, based on the work of Carolyn Downey and colleagues (Downey, Steffy, English, Frase, & Poston, 2004). They are structured and require that the observer be watchful for several things:

- student engagement (orientation)
- instructional goals
- activities that students are expected to be doing
- teacher's decisions and teaching practices
- levels of thinking required of students (according to Bloom's taxonomy)
- safety issues
- use of physical space in classroom ("walking the walls")

We also look for examples of differentiation, although we don't always see clear examples of differentiation during a five-minute observation. Figure 3.1 provides a sample of the 8 × 5 index card on which we each take notes when we do our walk-throughs.

In our district, administrators are expected to conduct regular walk-throughs of the classrooms in their buildings. Walk-throughs are also the first part of our administrative PLC meetings. We break into groups of two or three administrators and do walk-throughs of two or three classrooms

FIGURE 3.1 Walk-Through Card

| Name _____ Time _____ Student Orientation Y N |
| School: OHS OJHS H S L Subject/Grade _____ Date _____ |

Content/Objective (what is being taught)	Safety
Context (the givens; nature of student response)	Instruction (teacher practices)
Cognitive Level (Bloom's) Knowledge　　　Analysis　　　Application Comprehension　Synthesis　　Evaluation	Walk the Walls

in the building hosting that particular PLC meeting. Afterward, we debrief together. Below is a bit of transcript from a debriefing after two administrators (Kim and Dan) did a walk-through of a seventh-grade honors math class. The excerpt starts with Kim and Dan discussing which levels of Bloom's taxonomy they observed during the walk-through. Our administrative team has a strong collegial culture, and we enjoy friendly verbal jousts. While we learn together, we also have fun together.

Kim: I think the approach our math teachers use—the investigative or inquiry-based approach—utilizes inherently some analysis because the kids have to figure out what's going on in the pattern they are seeing, and then they have to synthesize that into an algorithm or formula that they can then use for future, new situations. So in a way, the part that we saw was probably more about comprehension, but the bigger picture, what he was trying to do with these kids, sort of moved around within Bloom's taxonomy. What do you think?

Dan: Yeah, I agree with you there, but even within just the five-minute segment that we saw, he was taking some of the knowledge or the comprehension that they had just three or four minutes ago and applying it into that next step.

Kim: OK, I see what you are saying. But it wasn't a completely novel, new situation to which they were applying previous learning, right?

Dan: No, right, right.

[As Dan and Kim continue their debriefing, the conversation moves from the topic of Bloom's taxonomy to differentiation pedagogy.]

Dan: He also did a great job of explaining it in different ways—you know we focus quite a bit on differentiation, and he differentiated his styles or strategies that could be used to solve a problem on just the very basic problems, so he showed there were two different ways to get the same answer.

Kim: Oh, true, he did do that, that's a good point. I also made a note that he uses an informal approach with the students; he speaks informally to them, more in a conversational tone. And I also wrote that he uses humor, and I think that goes back to his style—that's sort of who he is as a teacher, what he brings to the classroom, and I agree with you that that informal, humorous approach seems to work very well with the students. I too put that he was doing some demos on the board and that he, I think, is intentional about his use of different colors of whiteboard markers for different things. But seeing as you are color-blind, that probably flew right over your head as do many things, right? (Grins.)

Dan: (Laughs.) Double true. How about what the students were doing?...

As administrators, our habit of doing walk-throughs and debriefing together afterward familiarizes us with classroom practice and develops our ability to observe and analyze instruction. It also helps us to develop a strong vocabulary for talking about teaching.

Artifact Sharing or Critical Friends Session

Administrators are expected to bring to each of our PLC meetings one example of differentiation from their building. The artifacts can be projects, assessments, assignments, or instructional activities. During our meeting, we do a show-and-tell of sorts about each artifact. This is a great opportunity for us to share and celebrate good things going on in our buildings, to develop a cache of strong examples of differentiation, and to share ideas between buildings. For example, at one of our meetings, an elementary principal shared a differentiated study of various novels conducted by her sixth-grade teachers. The junior high principal took copies of the project back to share with his language arts teachers—so they could get ideas from their elementary colleagues and understand what their future students had been doing in sixth grade.

Below is a short snippet from one of our meetings in which Joe, the high school principal at the time, explains a differentiated notebook assignment used by one of his biology teachers:

Joe: I've got two examples—both from biology classes; they're from Karen Harold. And the first one is one that she gave out really at the start of the school year, when she told the kids that they had to do quarterly notebooks, and I'll just pass those around. If you look down the middle there, you'll see that she gave the kids options as to how they could present their notebook and she explained to them what a C option would be, what a B option would be, and what an A option would be. And then she gave them choices: they could do a PowerPoint, they could do a notebook with dividers, or they could do any other thing that they could think of, any other creative thing they could think of. So she differentiated in terms of the method that the kids could use: they could use whatever suited their fancy. So that's one example.

Kim: That's cool. I like that in this, even in the description of this, she talks about the fact that she recognizes some people are notebook people and that some people are not notebook people and that she wants to accommodate as many learning styles as possible. I think that's really cool.

Joe: Right, she tells them that.

Gretchen: How does this fit into those three chapters we just read? [Gretchen is referring to *Fair Isn't Always Equal* by Rick Wormeli.]

Kim: That's a great question.

Kathy: I know. I was thinking about that.

Nance: Well, at least there is no "If you earn a D..."

Joe: D and F are not options.

As you can see from this verbal exchange, we are very candid with each other and not afraid to seek explanations and rationales for what we believe. We try to keep these discussions open and honest. In this particular snippet, the discussion organically moved from the artifact being shared to what we had read in preparation for this PLC meeting, which was several chapters from *Fair Isn't Always Equal: Assessing and Grading in the Differentiated Classroom*, by Rick Wormeli (2006). That doesn't always happen though; sometimes the artifact sharing doesn't touch on the book we've been studying. That's OK. Sharing artifacts helps us to get a better sense of what differentiation looks like in classrooms and gives us a cache of examples that we can share with teachers and parents.

Critical Friends is a process for group reflection and problem-solving. We use the consultancy protocol, which centers around a presenter sharing an issue or challenge that she is experiencing in her leadership role. The discussants (other members of the PLC) ask probing and clarifying questions and then provide feedback and ideas to the presenter. "Warm" feedback is positive and supportive; "cool" feedback raises questions or provides alternative ways of thinking about or approaching the challenge; "hard" feedback raises concerns and challenges the presenter's thinking. The presenter then reflects aloud to the whole group on what she heard and learned from their input. This protocol includes a specific time limit for each step of the process. A facilitator (another member of the PLC) reviews the process at the beginning of the session, makes sure time limits are honored (or gently revised as needed), participates in the discussion, and leads the debriefing process at the end. For a concise, helpful guide to the Critical Friends process, go to http://depts.washington.edu/ccph/pdf_files/CriticalFriends.pdf.

For some members of our PLC, this is the most meaningful portion of the PLC. We have found that we get excellent ideas from the group and that a valuable synergy occurs: One discussant will have an idea or suggestion that another discussant adds to or builds upon. There's a beautiful give-and-take among the discussants. The Critical Friends protocol not only greatly helps us solve challenges that we are facing but also promotes a team mentality in our administrative group, encourages critical thinking and brainstorming, and promotes reflection. It reduces our isolation as administrators of a building or department and helps us feel that we are all on the same team and are there to help each other.

Our Critical Friends sessions have been so meaningful that we have agreed as a group to rally together on the spur of the moment if a colleague needs a spontaneous Critical Friends session to address a time-sensitive problem. On a number of occasions, members of our team have gathered in person or via conference call for an impromptu, informal Critical Friends process. We are all better leaders for it.

Book Study and Discussion

After we finish sharing and discussing our artifacts, we turn to our book discussion. Our PLC is constantly studying books about differentiation—for example, about leadership for differentiation or grading in a differentiated classroom. These books are a key way that we learn more about differentiation. We do activities to get us thinking, digesting, and reflecting on what we've read and how it applies to our schools. The transcript below is from a discussion of the aforementioned book, *Fair Isn't Always Equal*.

To begin the discussion, Kim provided each member of the PLC with six cards—five marked with a different letter of the grading scale (A, B, C, D, F) and one left blank. Kim explained that the purpose of this activity, borrowed from Wormeli, was to try to identify what we mean by these different letter grades—how we define them in our own heads. One card was left blank to encourage us to think outside of the traditional grading scale, adding something new to the grading scale such as a U or a star. We spent some time trying to define each letter grade on the cards; the discussion follows:

Kim: Let's start with the letter—the grade of—C. So who wants to share their C first? What do you have for your C there, Dan?

Dan: I wrote "Proficient knowledge of concepts."

Kim: OK.

Dan: And then I wrote a term that I don't really like. And I wouldn't accept it. "Middle of the road with concept understanding," but I can't tell you what middle of the road means.

Kim: Is that middle of the road as in average compared normatively?

Dan: Yeah, it's the average; average is the same thing as middle of the road. Yes, normatively middle of the road. It's kind of where, it's a general understanding, it's nothing exceptional, it's nothing great, it's an understanding though. If you are not at that D or F range, you understand the concept, but just at a very basic level. Basic might be a good word up there.

Kim: OK, I'm confused because the first part of that says proficient knowledge of concepts, so that's like a criterion referenced statement.

Dan: You have a proficient knowledge of the material that the teacher wanted you to learn.

Kim: OK. The second part though, the "middle of the road with concept understanding" sounds more norm referenced as opposed to criterion referenced. Because are you talking about kind of the average among the students or are you talking about a basic understanding of the content but nothing beyond basic? Because do you see what I am saying—that those are two different things?

Dan: Well, they are two different things and I told you that I didn't like it. The top one I'm fine with.

Kim: OK.

Nance: But I think mine is just like Dan's.

Kim: Oh, really?

Nance: I do.

Dan: That's because you were sitting next to me and you copied. (Grins.)

Nance: That's what C is for. Copy. (Grins.) I just have "you meet and know the standards." You know, you understand the basic information and concepts that are presented but your work is more average—it doesn't show application, it doesn't—you know—show some of those higher skills.

Kim: OK.

Dan: There are so many different views. You look at this book and this guy is considered an expert.

Gretchen: Right.

Dan: Well, I don't agree with everything he says.

Kim: Neither do I.

Gretchen: Right.

Dan: And I'm certain that our staff, each of our staff members, will have different views from our views and from his, and that there will be some combination there.

Gretchen: But I just think to start the conversation again...

After our study of Wormeli's book, several of our administrators decided to share parts of the book with their faculties and then discuss them at faculty meetings.

Our PLC has also studied some other wonderful books and videos about differentiation, including the following:

- Kingore, B. (2004). *Differentiation: Simplified, Realistic, and Effective*. Austin, TX: Professional Associates Publishing.
- Tomlinson, C. A., Demirsky Allan, S. (2000). *Leadership for Differentiating Schools & Classrooms*. Alexandria, VA: ASCD.
- *Differentiated Instruction in Action*. (2008). DVD Three Disc Series. ASCD.
- *A Visit to a School Moving Toward Differentiation*. (2007). DVD with Viewer's Guide. ASCD.

We have also been using some books about leadership more broadly, including:

- Reeves, D. (2009). *Leading Change in Your School: How to Conquer Myths, Build Commitment, and Get Results*. Alexandria, VA: ASCD.

These lists are by no means exhaustive of the types of texts that can be valuable for an administrative PLC.

Benefits and Byproducts of Our Administrative PLC

We started our administrative PLC primarily to increase our own knowledge of differentiation and to do what we were encouraging our teachers to do. We have found, though, some interesting byproducts and benefits of our PLC:

- *Common vocabulary*: We are developing a shared vocabulary around differentiation that we try to utilize within our schools so that everyone in the district is speaking the same language.
- *Credibility as instructional leaders*: We now know a fair amount about differentiation, and that gives us "street cred" in our buildings. Additionally, thanks to our walk-throughs, we are familiar with

what's going on in our buildings and are getting better at analyzing and discussing instruction. And thanks to our artifact sharing, we are able to give our staffs examples of many top-quality differentiated assessments, assignments, projects, and activities.
- *Confidence*: We feel more confident talking to our teachers and parents about differentiation. We feel more confident analyzing and speaking intelligently about what we see going on in classrooms.
- *Increased collegiality*: As a team, we have grown closer through our PLC—eating together, learning together, and laughing together. While it's very hard to carve out time from our schedules each month, once we get together, we enjoy and value our time together.
- *Knowledge of our schools*: Since we rotate the location of our meetings each month, we get to know not only our own buildings better through our walk-throughs and artifact sharing, but also each other's buildings. This gives us a better sense of our district holistically beyond our own building and helps us connect what's going on at the elementaries to the junior high and the senior high.
- *Commiseration*: It can be cathartic and restorative to have sympathetic ears listen to us, and we greatly value the chance to vent and release our frustrations to those who understand.
- *Pride and momentum*: Walk-throughs and artifact sharing have built pride in us about the good things going on in the district. Our schools' successes encourage and inspire us and propel us forward to do more.

Creating Your Own PLC

Hopefully these last several pages have inspired you to create your own PLC. This section offers advice for creating your own PLC, based on what we've learned along the way.

- Base your PLC on common goals shared across the district. A building or district should focus its primary energy on stated, impactful, meaningful goals. Doing a PLC for the sake of doing a PLC will not be as effective as doing a PLC as a way to achieve a broader, common goal (like enculturating differentiation). Tying a PLC to an important goal gives it gravitas.
- Find texts and other resources (books or videos) to use as a core text for the group. A core text helps to center a PLC and provide a common knowledge base from which to grow and discuss.

- Whether you're in a big or little district, create a *small* team of *diverse* building leaders. Our district is little, so our building and district administrators are in one PLC. It's important to keep PLCs small—no more than six or seven participants. Bigger districts could form a team based on building clusters (e.g., administrators of buildings feeding a specific high school) or a group of elementary administrators only (who have diverse educational philosophies or backgrounds). Another option is to form administrative PLCs based on a certain topic or text. In this model, large districts may have four or more different administrative PLCs—each based on a different core text or subtopic of differentiation (e.g., assessment and grading)—comprised of a mix of administrators.
- Outline meetings and assignments before beginning the school year. Each year, Kim makes bookmarks for us that contain all our meeting dates, with location and reading assignment for each. We just stick the bookmark into our core text. We've learned that it's important to have a plan from the start of a year. Otherwise, a plan never seems to develop.
- Rotate meeting locations and hosting duties. This is a great way to get into each other's buildings to get ideas and become more familiar with the district as a whole. And we *always* have snacks or treats at our meetings. There is something about eating together that is itself a bonding thing.
- Identify a facilitator and split or rotate the facilitator's duties. Shared group leadership is key to engaging all participants as learners and leaders. Kim heads up the overall planning of the group, but each of us takes turns leading a meeting—particularly the book discussion part of the meeting.

Summary

To successfully lead a building or district toward enculturating differentiation, leaders must be knowledgeable about differentiation. We believe that the best way to become more knowledgeable and to develop a supportive leadership network is to form an administrative professional learning community. In this chapter, we have tried to give you a peek into our own PLC and to provide suggestions for those who are interested in starting their own administrative PLC.

References

Downey, C. J., Steffy, B. E., English, F.W., Frase, L. E., & Poston, W. K. (2004). *The three-minute classroom walk-through: Changing school supervisory practice one teacher at a time.* Thousand Oaks, CA: Corwin Press.

Schlechty, P. C. (1993). On the frontier of school reform with trailblazers, pioneers, and settlers. *Journal of Staff Development*, 14(4), 46–51.

Southwest Educational Development Laboratory. (1997). Professional learning communities: What are they and why are they important? *Issues . . . about Change*, 6(1), 1–8.

Wormeli, R. (2006). *Fair isn't always equal: Assessing and grading in the differentiated classroom.* Portland, ME: Stenhouse.

4
Beckoning: "Light" Strategies

> **This chapter will**
>
> 1. introduce Carol Ann Tomlinson's metaphor of fire and light for cultivating differentiation in every classroom
> 2. identify strategies to *draw* teachers toward change, including teacher leadership, modeling, professional development, and celebration

"Differentiation is not an invitation; it is an expectation."
—Oakwood City School District CORE Team

"My knee-jerk reaction [to being required to differentiate instruction] was, 'You can't make me.' It was your standard, middle-aged, white guy rant . . . The PLCs were a good strategy for me. I shut my big mouth and learned from colleagues, people I respect. They've given me a broad range of perspectives."
—Rob Guizzo, 35-year veteran
Oakwood High School science teacher

Fire and Light Metaphor

This chapter introduces the reader to a "fire and light" metaphor used by Carol Ann Tomlinson to emphasize the need to both draw and push educators toward differentiation. This chapter also goes into detail about "light" strategies that can be used by leaders to effect change for differentiation. Chapter 5 will focus on "fire" strategies that push teachers toward change for differentiation.

In 2007, Carol Ann Tomlinson presented a session titled "Differentiation and Change: Fiddlers on the Schoolhouse Roof" at the annual ASCD conference. During the presentation, she introduced the metaphor of fire and light as paramount to a school's or district's efforts to cultivate differentiation in every classroom.

Light symbolizes efforts to beckon and draw teachers toward change. Light represents warmth, companionship, comfort, and security. Comfort and security are not often associated with change efforts, but light strategies can provide them. Such strategies, which will be discussed in the following sections, include teacher leadership, modeling, professional development, and celebration.

Light strategies have the greatest impact, and most of a school's or district's efforts should be invested in beckoning and drawing educators toward change. Not all teachers, however, respond to being beckoned by the light. Fire strategies are therefore necessary to communicate that all teachers are *expected* to differentiate and that this expectation is *nonnegotiable*.

Fire symbolizes the necessity of making it uncomfortable—or impossible—for teachers to maintain the status quo. Fire makes us uncomfortably hot and forces us to move away from where we are. This is critical because, as the Oakwood mantra says, differentiation is not an invitation; it is an expectation. Fire strategies include differentiated supervision, aligning teacher evaluation to differentiation, and providing "required choice" professional development. These strategies are discussed in the next chapter.

Neither cajoling nor forcing people to change is particularly effective (Reeves, 2009). Change is a messy, complicated, and often confounding process. We believe, however, that when both light and fire strategies are infused into a school's or district's change initiative, change is more likely not only to occur but to become part of a school's or district's culture.

While there are perhaps innumerable light strategies, the four that we believe are most effective are teacher leadership, modeling, professional development, and celebration.

Teacher Leadership

We have learned that teachers are more likely to follow the lead of fellow teachers whom they respect than they are to follow administrators or outside experts. One of the best examples of teacher leadership within our district is our CORE Team. (CORE is not an acronym; the full word is capitalized to show the importance of the group's role.) The CORE Team was established in 2005 in order to lead the differentiation change process. The team is composed of eight teachers from across the district, two principals, and our curriculum director. As curriculum director, Kim asked principals and other teacher leaders within the district (e.g., the district's professional development committee, which is discussed later in this chapter) for recommendations of teachers who embodied teacher leadership and who were early adopters of differentiation. The recommended teachers were respected and admired by their peers, who had credibility and capital among their peers. Kim personally invited each recommended teacher to participate on the CORE Team.

Initially, the team met to negotiate what we mean by differentiation, what, exactly, our vision for differentiation is, and how best to implement the vision. The CORE Team developed the differentiation self-assessment rubric for teachers (see Figure 5.2), initiated professional learning communities (PLCs), and developed the mantra "Differentiation is not an invitation; it is an expectation." It was this team that identified the necessity of using not only light strategies to draw people toward differentiation but also fire strategies to push people toward differentiation by making the status quo uncomfortable. The CORE Team also helped to develop the Differentiation Choice Board used as part of our teacher evaluation system (see Figure 5.3), which is discussed in Chapter 5.

♦ ♦ ♦ ♦ ♦ ♦ ♦ ♦ ♦
Oakwood's Differentiation Vision:

All Oakwood teachers will regularly differentiate content, process, and product for student readiness, interests, and strengths.

♦ ♦ ♦ ♦ ♦ ♦ ♦ ♦ ♦

Since that first year, the CORE Team has met at least annually to evaluate our district's progress toward its differentiation vision and to identify steps to further that progress and to keep change momentum going. The three greatest contributions of this group have been its role in bringing PLCs to our district, its role in tying teacher evaluation to differentiation, and—perhaps most important of all—its role in modeling the best of professionalism, its commitment to doing right by students and to expecting great things of their peers.

We have the greatest respect for this group of leaders for, without them, our district would not have made the gains that it has. We firmly believe that a team of teacher leaders (sprinkled with a few administrators) is key to planning, evaluating, and maintaining momentum in making differentiation part of the school or district culture.

Modeling

Paramount in a change initiative for differentiation is to walk the walk and not just talk the talk. If we as administrators want differentiation to become part of the school or district culture, then by all means we must model differentiation ourselves and participate in professional development to help us do so. What does this mean? What does this modeling look like?

1. *Administrative PLC*: As described in Chapter 3, all our building administrators, as well as our curriculum director and superintendent, participate in the administrative PLC. By reading, learning, and growing together, we not only strengthen our individual leadership skills and our group's closeness and strength, but we also model our commitment to learning in general and to PLCs and differentiation in particular.
2. *Differentiated professional development*: All our professional development (PD) is differentiated. Our PLCs are differentiated by topic, target audience, and format. Our PD days offer a variety of concurrent choice sessions that differ by target audience, readiness level (e.g., beginner, intermediate, and advanced sessions about SMART Board and its classroom applications), topics (reflecting teachers' differing interests), and length or depth (some sessions are a single block; some are half-day; some are full-day). Teachers also have the option on our PD days of participating in site visits, which are trips to other schools or districts, attractions such as art, history, or science museums, or other organizations, such as the University of Dayton anatomy lab.
3. *Routine administrative practices*: We always look for opportunities to model differentiation in our regular administrative activities. For example, at a recent two-day, K–12, science vertical alignment event, we used activities and materials that spoke to visual, auditory, and tactile modalities and provided participants their choice of reflection activities differentiated for linear and divergent thinkers.

4. *Differentiated supervision and evaluation*: We use a supervision and evaluation approach, discussed in the next chapter, that evaluates teacher differentiation and at the same time is itself differentiated.

Each time we as administrators model differentiation, we are saying that we value differentiation and are committed to it.

Professional Development

In order for differentiation to be woven into the cultural fabric of a school or district, educators need to know what it is, how to do it, how to manage it, and how to assess it. Professional development is therefore crucial. Here are some professional development opportunities that we offer:

1. Professional learning communities (PLCs): PLCs are collegial groups of educators who are united in their commitment to student learning and who meet together regularly to learn about and focus on a topic. Benefits to the staff and students include reduced isolation of teachers, increased collegiality, better informed and more committed teachers, and academic gains for students (SEDL, 1997). In Oakwood, our PLC facilitators are fellow teachers who volunteer to serve as organizers and leaders of the PLCs. They are not expected to be differentiation gurus. Their role includes selecting the focus of the PLC (e.g., differentiation in the elementary math classroom; writing workshop; obstacles to differentiation and strategies for overcoming them in high school classrooms), the core text for the PLC, the target audience, and the meeting dates and times of the group. Some Oakwood PLCs meet before school, some during our lunch hour (we enjoy a full noninstructional hour for lunch), and some after school. Groups meet at least once a month, and we require a one-year commitment to PLCs. Each September we distribute to teachers a booklet listing the PLCs that will be offered during that school year. Participation in PLCs is strictly voluntary. The nonnegotiables for PLCs are as follows:

- PLCs are all focused on some aspect of differentiation (e.g., analyzing student work to inform differentiated instruction, developing differentiated units of study, the implications of differentiation for grading).
- PLCs should be action-oriented, since their purpose is to help teachers put differentiation into action.

- PLCs should be emotionally safe places where teachers feel collegial support and are free to take professional risks.

PLCs have been the most impactful and important professional development opportunities that we have offered in Oakwood. Rob Guizzo, the veteran science teacher quoted at the beginning of this chapter, credits the PLCs he has participated in with changing his attitude and helping him to implement differentiation in his science classroom. For Rob, the PLCs provided a "climate of professional respect" that was "very accepting, very collegial," making him feel "less threatened and more inclined to try" differentiation strategies. His PLCs helped Rob to see that a teacher could "incorporate [differentiation] with who you are and what you do. You don't have to throw out all you do and start over . . . For an old dog despairing of learning too many new tricks, the collegial atmosphere" of PLCs offered him a safe place to take risks and to experience "minimum pain for gain." For Rob, PLCs have been "much better than visiting presenters" at helping him to feel comfortable with change toward differentiation. Rob's experience is profound; he has identified one of the most important elements of PLCs: By providing emotionally and intellectually safe places among caring, committed peers, PLCs provide the "ontological security" needed to face change (Starratt, 1993). To some degree, change always requires moving away from what we know and feel comfortable with and moving toward something that is foreign and uncertain. This process risks our ontological security, our comfort and certainty in what we know to be real and true, and causes anxiety:

> If we do not know what to do, and furthermore, other people know that we do not know what to do, then we feel separated from "reality." Our anxiety over losing our sense of competency and autonomy triggers resistance to untried and uncertain routines and urges return to those familiar routines which have worked in the past. (Starratt, 1993, pp. 34–35)

The caring, committed, collegial nature of PLCs—in which everyone is a learner taking risks—reduces anxiety that educators have about feeling competent in differentiation. PLCs help to support colleagues' ontological security as they meet change.

Below are a few PLCs that we have offered in Oakwood.

♦ ♦ ♦ ♦ ♦ ♦ ♦ ♦ ♦

PLC 301: Implementing Writing Workshop Using Write Traits II

Facilitated by: Monica Brouwer
Target Audience: Elementary Writing Teachers
Meetings: TBD (Bring your calendar on Oct. 17)

Did you know that Writing Workshop is a great way to differentiate writing instruction? Have you thought about implementing Writing Workshop in your classroom but don't know where to start? In this PLC we will continue to explore the ins and outs of Writing Workshop. We will work through management strategies, share ideas for mini-lessons, and learn ways to incorporate Write Traits into Writing Workshop.

This PLC is a follow-up to last year's and welcomes both new and returning members.

PLC 302: Teaching Essentials

Facilitated by: Susan Lang and Elizabeth Myers
Target Audience: Elementary Teachers at Smith and Harman
Meetings: TBD (Bring your calendar Oct. 17!)
Participants will receive a free copy of *Teaching Essentials* by Routman

We've spent the last few years building "pieces" of our day with differentiation. How do we put all the pieces together? To work on integrating differentiation into our day and improving our overall practice, we will look at *Teaching Essentials* by Regie Routman. A well-respected author, Routman looks at the essential elements of sound teaching practice. We will share both Routman's ideas as well as our own. Hope to see you there!

PLC 303: Technology as a Teaching Tool

Facilitated by: Brianna Doyal
Target Audience: Teachers at OJHS/OHS
Meetings: TBD (Bring your calendar on Oct. 17!)

Interested in exploring how technology can help you differentiate instruction? Have ideas on what to use technology for, but don't know *how* to make it happen? Want to know how your peers are using technology in their classrooms? Focused on finding fast and simple ways to apply the tools the district already owns, this PLC is your opportunity to collaborate with peers as we explore how technology can be used as a tool for enhancing our classroom instruction. All skill levels welcome . . . all you need are ideas!

PLC 304: Science: A Different Approach

Facilitated by: Kim Hobby and Heidi Steinbrink
Target Audience: OJHS/OHS Science Teachers
Meetings: During the lunch hour (Bring your calendar on Oct. 17!)
Participants will utilize copies of *Misconceptions in the Science Classroom* **and** *Uncovering Student Ideas in Science (I, II, III)*.

Labs. Safety. Content. Technology. Standards. The demands in the science classroom are ongoing, so how do you fit differentiation into your instruction as well? This PLC will help you to differentiate within the science classroom, while still working to meet all content goals. A focus of this group will be to examine how to differentiate similar content across grade bands and courses at the junior high and senior high level. With a concentration on enriching curriculum, bring your ideas and let's work together to improve our teaching and our ability to reach our kids with the richest classroom experience possible. This PLC will be a collaboration of ideas to brainstorm and create usable lessons and activities for the classroom. So if you want materials to put into practice, this PLC is for you!

◆ ◆ ◆ ◆ ◆ ◆ ◆ ◆ ◆

2. Professional development day sessions by internal and external presenters: Each academic year, we have two full-day district professional development days. Usually, these days consist of four blocks of time during each of which about twelve concurrent choice sessions are held for our 160 or so teachers and paraprofessionals. The district's professional development committee (PDC) plans these days. PDC is comprised of teacher representatives from buildings and two administrators. Some of the presenters PDC selects for our professional development days are internal—our own teachers—and some are experts external to our district. Not all of our professional development day sessions are related to differentiation. Below are a few descriptions of sessions offered at our professional development days:

◆ ◆ ◆ ◆ ◆ ◆ ◆ ◆ ◆ ◆

Special Learners in the Music Classroom: Differentiating Music Instruction for Inclusion

Audience: K–12 Music Teachers, Aides, and Administrators
Session Leader: Dr. Susan Gardstrom, coordinator of the music therapy degree program at the University of Dayton

This session, led by Dr. Susan Gardstrom, focuses on differentiation and adaptation of the music classroom for students with special needs. The session provides specific strategies for accommodating and modifying the learning environment, materials, and instructional procedures to meet students' learning needs.

K-W-L on Collaboration and Co-Teaching

Audience: K–12 Teachers, Aides, and Administrators
Session Leaders: Crystal Melchor and Elizabeth Fasig

This informative, interactive session, based on Dr. Wendy Murawski's Bureau of Education & Research workshop, will clarify co-teaching and collaboration. Key components and definitions of both will be presented as well as benefits. Participants will learn co-teaching approaches, do's and don'ts, and leave with a step-by-step plan to achieve a co-teaching environment.

How to Manage the Pool with Michael Phelps and the Dog Paddler: Sink or Swim for Differentiation

Audience: 3–8 Teachers
Session Leaders: Kim Walther, Amy Williams, Amanda Ammer, and Melody Knostman

We recently returned from an ASCD institute on differentiation with Carol Ann Tomlinson. Join us as we dive into some practical new ideas and strategies for differentiating instruction in your classroom. We will wrap up our session with some fun organizational give-aways! Yes, that means free stuff!

◆ ◆ ◆ ◆ ◆ ◆ ◆ ◆ ◆ ◆

3. Outside workshops and conferences: In addition to planning our district's two annual professional development days, PDC is charged with determining funding for teachers who apply to attend conferences and workshops outside the district. Recently, four of our teachers (three gifted intervention specialists and one elementary teacher) attended a two-day ASCD institute on differentiation led by Carol Ann Tomlinson. Upon their return, the teachers designed a session they titled "How to Manage the Pool with Michael Phelps and the Dog Paddler: Sink or Swim for Differentiation" (described above) for our professional development day. This is a highly encouraged and effective way to spread learning throughout the district and to leverage limited financial resources.

4. Pizza & PD sessions: These are after-school events, from 3:45 to 5:30 p.m., targeted for 5 to 15 attendees who enjoy pizza and drinks while discussing very specific, very practical topics that are intended to be immediately applicable to classroom instruction. Here are a few examples:

♦ ♦ ♦ ♦ ♦ ♦ ♦ ♦ ♦

Differentiated Spelling in the Elementary Classroom: Tips, Tricks and Tools for Implementation and Management

Facilitated by: Pamela Ellis
Target Audience: Elementary Language Arts Teachers

This session will provide teachers with practical ideas and tools for differentiating spelling instruction in the elementary classroom. It will combine a developmental approach with the district-adopted Rebecca Sitton Program. Teachers will receive sample assessments and classroom tools that they can take with them and use in their classrooms.

Clickers: Developing, Finding, and Efficiently Utilizing SMART Response Question Sets

Facilitated by: Jon Rowley
Target Audience: All Teachers and Staff

Come learn the ins and outs of developing question sets for student response systems (clickers). Creating question sets from scratch will be a focus. Participants will also learn how to access and utilize available question sets that have already been created by teachers all over the world. Finally, we will explore "on the fly" question set templates that require minimal pre-lesson preparation. This technique allows the teacher to create or adjust questions mid-lesson in order to meet the needs of students.

Cooperative Learning

Facilitated by: Kelly Colson
Target Audience: Teachers of Grades K–12

This session is for you if you are looking for some new, easy-to-implement strategies for making cooperative learning really work in your classroom. We will talk about a variety of cooperative learning topics including fun ways to group your students, cooperative learning processing activities, strategies for engaging all members of a group, and more!

♦ ♦ ♦ ♦ ♦ ♦ ♦ ♦ ♦

5. **Summer and winter institutes through partnership with Centerville:** Oakwood is a small district. One of the ways that we try to maximize our professional development offerings to teachers is through a partnership that we have established with Centerville City School District. Centerville is a neighboring district that is much larger than Oakwood and has far greater financial resources than we do. Through the partnership, our teachers have access to all the sessions offered by the summer and winter institutes that Centerville provides. Centerville's professional development focus—"Whatever It Takes: Examining Approaches, Methods, and Strategies to Meet the Needs of All Learners with 'Best Practices'"—is really differentiation in fancy wording. Thus Centerville's focus and Oakwood's commitment to differentiation are a perfect match.

Celebration

Acts of celebration honor the dignity and importance of educators who take risks in order to achieve differentiation. Large and small, public and private acts of celebration are ways of valuing the heart, guts, and effort that teachers devote to implementing differentiation. Celebration also serves the purpose of maintaining momentum during the long and laborious process of change.

> The challenge to leaders is to create an institutional environment in which both the employees and the clients experience something approaching that sense of personal importance and dignity which are experienced in the home and neighborhood. It will not work if it is simply a human relations ploy; it must be connected to the spirit and meaning of the organization itself. (Starratt, 1993, p. 40)

Each school and district has its own unique culture. In Oakwood, the culture is such that forms of celebration that call out individual teachers, through rituals such as Teacher of the Month, are not only unwelcome but seen as divisive. The forms of celebration that we use respect Oakwood's culture by focusing on specific, tangible good things that educators are doing for students rather than grandstanding individual educators. We thus reinforce our district's mission of "doing what's best for students." The following are some examples of celebration. We encourage other schools and districts to find ways to celebrate that honor their own cultures.

1. School and district newsletter blurbs: Oakwood High School principal Paul Waller asks each of his department chairs to write short blurbs for the school's monthly newsletter for parents. While one purpose of the blurbs is to keep parents informed about instructional matters, this is also a way for teachers, administrators, parents, and students to learn about our teachers' efforts to "do what's best for students." Here's an example:

Math Department News:
"Design a House": Students in Math 1 classes are currently researching houses, building materials, and scale drawings. The students will be creating scale drawings for a three-bedroom house and comparing costs for the building materials. Students will also investigate the cost and benefits of using "green" building materials. This project will allow students to reinforce and use a real-world application of their course work in ratios, proportions, and data analysis. This project will be completed with the science department where the students will build the scale model.

Even though it is not explicitly called out in the blurb, these freshman-level college prep classes are using cooperative groups, a process differentiation strategy, in this project. There are other elements of quality instruction in play, including constructivist teaching practices, real-world application of learning, and project-based learning. This example demonstrates how differentiation can be woven together with other research-based practices.

2. Principals' "weeklies": Every week Oakwood principals send to faculty and staff a short email announcing schedule changes, upcoming important events, and great things going on in classrooms. The following example comes from

Dan, the principal of Oakwood Junior High, whose staff weeklies contain a "Did You Know" section that celebrates myriad happenings around the building:

Did You Know???
Kim Gilbert has been working diligently on a differentiation flip chart for all of us to use. This will be an excellent tool when it is finished. Great job, Kim.

English and language arts teacher Kim Gilbert was inspired by an online class that she took to author a flip chart on differentiation strategies, including the title of each strategy, an example of the strategy in action, and how it embodies differentiation. The chart is being made available to all Oakwood teachers.

3. Curriculum showcases at board meetings: At each of our district's monthly board meetings, we offer a 10-minute presentation on some aspect of our curricular or professional development offerings. Generally, when educators lead a curriculum showcase, they use photos, video or audio clips, demonstrations, student work samples, or an overview of equipment to help the board learn more about the program or project being highlighted. We encourage presenters to include students as part of the presentation. Here is an example of a curriculum showcase as described in Oakwood's *Boardlines*:

Rube Goldberg, the famous engineer, inventor, and cartoonist, won the Pulitzer Prize in 1948 for his cartoons depicting what have become known as Rube Goldberg machines—overly complex and complicated machines designed to complete simple tasks, such as turning a coin over from one side to the other. Mr. Bill Tant will share with the Board several of the Rube Goldberg machines designed by his eighth-grade students. The Goldberg project was inquiry-based and differentiated in multiple ways: students could choose whether to work independently or with a group; they could select their own task for their machine to accomplish; and they could select their own materials for and design their own machine. Mr. Tant's students will share with the Board the Goldberg machines that they designed.

4. Thank-you notes: This year, we purchased bushels of blank thank-you cards that our CORE Team distributed at faculty meetings and placed in front offices and faculty rooms. Educators were invited to write a thank-you card to celebrate or recognize a colleague's contributions. The purpose behind the cards was to show that we value each other professionally and to build our sense of shared identity.

5. Kudos emails: As administrators, we try to personally recognize the contributions of faculty and staff via individual, short emails showing our appreciation. Here is an example that Kim sent to two teachers, Rob Guizzo and Rachel Keyes, who led a Pizza & PD after-school session on online math and science simulations known as Gizmos (a great way to differentiate science instruction for tactile learners and students interested in technology). Kim sent a copy of her email to each teacher's principal and to the superintendent as well:

Rob and Rachel:
I just wanted to drop you a quick email to tell you how impressed I was with your Pizza & PD session today on Gizmos.

You were incredibly well prepared. It was obvious that you put a good deal of thought, time, and planning into your session. I also like the graphic organizer that you handed out for note-taking. You handled the tech problems with the server being down with aplomb and went on with your Plan B until those issues could be worked out. You were both enthusiastic and engaging. You worked very well together. I enjoyed learning more about Gizmos and getting to try one out for myself. They are very cool. GREAT job! I hope that you can repeat your session again sometime.

—Kim

Celebrating educators' differentiation efforts in ways that are culturally appropriate for your school will communicate the value that you place on teachers, improve the climate of the building, reinforce teachers' commitment to differentiation, and keep the change momentum going.

Summary

Light strategies are effective means of *drawing* or *attracting* educators toward change for differentiation. Such strategies include, but are certainly not limited to, teacher leadership, modeling, professional development, and celebration. The next chapter shifts the focus to fire strategies that push educators toward change.

References

Reeves, D. (2009). *Leading change in your school: How to conquer myths, build commitment, and get results*. Alexandria, VA: ASCD.
Southwest Educational Development Laboratory. (1997). Professional learning communities: What are they and why are they important? *Issues . . . about Change*, 6(1), 1–8.
Starratt, R. J. (1993). *The drama of leadership*. London: Falmer Press.

5

Pushing: "Fire" Strategies

> ***This chapter will***
>
> 1. identify strategies to *push* teachers toward change, including differentiating supervision, aligning teacher evaluation to differentiation, and providing "required choice" professional development
> 2. debunk the "just a little bit better is good enough" myth by drawing on Doug Reeves's work and discussing the implications for differentiation change
> 3. introduce the reader to Doug Reeves's "Toxic 2" and discuss its implications for change initiatives

A Personal Anecdote from Kim...

Two cavities! Yikes! I was shocked. The dentist declared that these two cavities—located between two of my teeth—were due to lack of flossing. Ooops.

Let's be honest—I've never been a big flosser. Despite my dentist's and hygienist's semiannual reminders and admonitions at my checkups to floss daily—and the little box of floss they gave me each visit—I didn't do it. I knew that I should. Doing so has always been in the best interest of my teeth. And I always had good intentions of increasing the frequency of my flossing, but it never seemed to stick. Then I had those two cavities filled. In the big scheme of life, it wasn't a horrendous experience, but it was just the kick in the pants that I needed to change. Now I floss daily. Faithfully.

In the anecdote above, Kim didn't change her flossing habits in response to the "light" strategies used by her dentist and hygienist—their reminders and admonitions about flossing and the floss they gave her. She resisted the change, even though she knew flossing was best for her teeth. It took an uncomfortable situation—getting two cavities filled—to push her to change. This is the same concept behind the "fire" strategies that are the focus of this chapter.

"Fire" Strategies

In the last chapter, we introduced the reader to Tomlinson's "fire and light" metaphor for differentiation change. The metaphor highlights the complementary forces of pull and push. "Light" strategies are those that draw or pull teachers toward change for differentiation, while "fire" strategies are those that nudge or push educators toward change. In other words, fire strategies are those that make the status quo—or standing still—uncomfortable or unpalatable. Changing becomes less uncomfortable than not changing.

Lest you believe that having a few or some of your teachers differentiating regularly will effect significant change, consider this:

> In fact, in surprising research, we found that for many change initiatives, implementation that was moderate or occasional was no better than implementation that was completely absent. Only deep implementation had the desired effect on student achievement. (Reeves, 2009, p. 44)

Implementation of differentiation, like any change initiative, must be deep and widespread. This is exactly why light strategies are crucially important and necessary to draw teachers toward the change and also why they are insufficient. Implementation, ultimately, must occur across the board, and that is why fire strategies are essential: We cannot avoid the "difficult truth that behavior precedes belief—that is, most people must engage in a behavior before they accept that it is beneficial; then they see the results, and then they believe that it is the right thing to do" (Reeves, 2009, p. 44). In other words, "implementation precedes buy-in" (p. 44). Therein lies the necessity of fire strategies that make avoiding the change initiative and holding tight to the status quo uncomfortable if not impossible.

As discussed in the last chapter, light strategies should receive most of a school's or district's attention, devotion, and resources. Nonetheless, fire strategies are needed to clearly and powerfully articulate to educators that differentiation is an *expectation*. It is *nonnegotiable*. It must happen because it is what is best for students.

While there are perhaps numerous fire strategies available to leaders, those that serve as the focus of this chapter are differentiated supervision, teacher evaluation tied to differentiation, and "required choice" professional development.

Differentiated Supervision

In *SuperVision and Instructional Leadership* (2001), Glickman, Gordon, and Ross-Gordon promote a continuum of supervision, from directive through collaborative to nondirective. Some teachers need more specific, structured direction (directive supervision), others need a cooperative approach based on frank conversations and mutual agreement on a plan of action (collaborative supervision), while still others are quite autonomous in their ability to self-reflect, identify areas for growth, and map out a plan of action. With this last type, the role of the supervisor is to "assist the teacher in the process of thinking through his or her actions" (p. 183) through nondirective supervision. Many principals could list teachers whose needs fit each of these categories.

Educators who need a directive approach require a clearly spelled out plan of action and improvement with a timeline of measurable objectives. While all educators who are at risk of being nonrenewed would fall into this category, not everyone in this category is at risk of being nonrenewed. Rather, people in this category are those who require an explicitly directed approach in order to successfully resolve problems and grow as educators.

What follows are two examples from Oakwood. The first is from an improvement plan developed through the directive approach. The second is an excerpt from a kindergarten teacher's professional goals developed through the nondirective approach.

◆ ◆ ◆ ◆ ◆ ◆ ◆ ◆ ◆

Inside Oakwood

Below is an excerpt from an improvement plan written for a department supervisor. The pseudonym "Johnson" has been used, and some details have been removed or changed to honor the privacy of the individual for whom it was written. This document reflects the directive approach to supervision.

1. **Ms. Johnson needs to improve her communication with her colleagues.**
   a. Ms. Johnson needs to understand her audience with all of her communications.
   b. Ms. Johnson will select the appropriate method for communicating (email, hard copy, telephone, in person, etc.) based upon timing and other factors in the situation.
   c. Ms. Johnson will be certain that her message (written or oral) is organized, clear, and understandable.
   d. Evidence of improvement in this area will be determined by:
      i. Sample pieces of communication
      ii. Feedback from stakeholders
2. **Ms. Johnson needs to involve building administrators in issues that affect their staff and/or buildings**
   a. Ms. Johnson will share her proposal of her 2007-2008 Budget with the Cabinet no later than February 15, 2008.
   b. Ms. Johnson will share her ideas with the Cabinet for how software and hardware should be approved, supported, and purchased no later than February 15, 2008.
   c. Ms. Johnson will continue to have open conversations with building administrators about their visions for her department's work in their buildings.
   d. Evidence of improvement in this area will be determined by:
      i. Budget Proposal by 2/15/08
      ii. Software/Hardware proposal by 2/15/08
      iii. Feedback from Administration Team
3. **Ms. Johnson needs to effectively prioritize and follow through on tasks that she has been asked/directed to do, or those that she says she will do.**
   a. Ms. Johnson will successfully coordinate district-wide professional development related to her department's area of responsibility.
      i. Calendar of classes, times, locations, and instructors will be submitted by February 1, 2008.
      ii. Ms. Johnson will also coordinate the promotion of these professional development opportunities.
      iii. Ms. Johnson will instruct some of the classes to build credibility among her colleagues.
      iv. Classes will occur each week, beginning no later than February 8, 2008.
      v. An accurate account of classes offered, dates, and names of attendees will be developed.

b. Ms. Johnson will take the Certification assessment for her position no later than January 30, 2008.
c. Evidence of improvement in this area will be determined by:
   i. Professional development schedule by 2/1/08, classes by 2/8/08, log of classes and attendees.
   ii. Ms. Johnson will earn her Certification.
   iii. For all tasks that Ms. Johnson is assigned or volunteers to do, she will keep a log. This log will contain: date initiated, task description, date completed, and priority level:
      1. 1 = Highest Priority—to be addressed immediately, perhaps completed before the end of the day or a specified time in the very near future.
      2. 2 = Medium Priority—not of immediate need, perhaps completed before the end of the week or a specified time in the not-too-distant future.
      3. 3 = Low Priority—perhaps a project or task that can be worked on over a break or during the summer. (If this is a task that someone has asked you to do, it is very important that you communicate with that individual when the task might get completed.)

It is recognized that Ms. Johnson is experiencing a significant learning curve in her new work environment this year, but there are many identified areas of weakness that must be addressed. It is very important for Ms. Johnson to begin working immediately on these areas of weakness. To review progress in these areas, a follow-up conference will be held at 2:00 PM on Friday, February 29, 2008 in the OJH office. A second follow-up conference will be held at 9:30 AM on Friday, March 14, 2008 in the OJH office.

The administration of Oakwood City Schools looks forward to observing significant improvement over the next two months.

♦ ♦ ♦ ♦ ♦ ♦ ♦ ♦ ♦

Figure 5.1 below shows a goal and action plan written autonomously by a veteran Oakwood kindergarten teacher. The nondirective supervision approach is most appropriate for this teacher.

What follows are the comments written by the teacher's supervisor assessing the teacher's goal attainment. This teacher required no direct support by her supervisor to attain her goals.

FIGURE 5.1 Goal and Action Plan for Kindergarten Teacher

Domain: Component	Performance Goal	Action Plan
1b 1d 3c	I would like to learn about and implement new techniques for working with students who learn best through kinesthetic modalities.	I plan to attend the class offered at Smith Elementary School for the Orton Gillingham approach (multisensory approach to reading instruction). Afterward, I plan to adapt and/or adopt those techniques that would be beneficial for kindergarten students. I plan to co-teach with Ashleigh Spencer, with her first modeling the strategies.

("Domain: Component" refers to the four domains of Charlotte Danielson's Framework for Teaching)

Margie did an excellent job of implementing and following through on her goal to utilize Orton Gillingham (OG) strategies to address the needs of tactile/kinesthetic learners. She attended professional development sessions on OG, co-taught with Intervention Specialist Ashleigh Spencer, and shared the strategies that she used with her colleagues. Additionally, Margie sought out information about S'Cool Moves and consulted with Occupational Therapist Ashley Banais about S'Cool Moves. Margie has implemented some of the S'Cool Moves strategies to help with sensory-motor integration, muscle endurance, and focus.

I greatly respect that Margie, with her many years of knowledge and expertise, strives to learn new strategies to address her students' needs. This speaks to her profound commitment to her students' success. Margie Cannard is a model of what a strong, experienced educator should be.

Why differentiate teacher supervision? Just as teachers are expected to differentiate for students' developmental readiness, so too are supervisors expected to differentiate for teachers' needs. We must differentiate our supervisory approach because it will best help teachers to grow, which in turn best helps students learn. Additionally, differentiating our supervisory approach also models for teachers the importance that leaders place on differentiation and our willingness to walk the walk and not just talk the talk.

By modeling our commitment to differentiation, we push ourselves, as leaders, as well as the educators we supervise into weaving differentiation into our school or district culture. Differentiation becomes ubiquitous, like the air that we breathe, and is obvious in the way we supervise.

Evaluating Teacher Differentiation and Differentiating Teacher Evaluation

The most obvious and most potent of the fire strategies that we have initiated is our teacher evaluation process. Like their counterparts in many schools and districts, Oakwood teachers go through the supervision cycle (preobservation conference, formal observation, postobservation conference, and follow-up) twice a year every one to three years, depending on their experience level. As part of each supervision cycle in Oakwood, the supervisor is expected to look for and assess the teacher's use of instructional technology and differentiation, in addition to the four domains of Charlotte Danielson's (2007) framework for teaching: (1) planning and preparation, (2) classroom environment, (3) instruction, and (4) professional responsibilities. This is a fairly common approach used in many schools and districts.

Additionally, all our teachers write their own professional goals annually. What is perhaps unique to Oakwood, however, is the requirement that one of those teacher goals *must* be related to differentiation. Also unique is the process through which the teacher goes to do this: The process is *itself* differentiated.

The CORE Team (see Chapter 4) was pivotal in the development of this rigorous process, which is outlined in the following paragraphs. We want to be clear that this process is an administrative requirement; administrators have the authority and power to *require* this process. The CORE Team, which provided the idea behind this process and shaped the content and format of the final documents, *supports* and helps teachers to write their differentiation goals. This difference in role is important. The CORE Team is composed mostly of teachers who serve to support and assist their peers and neither require nor conduct the actual evaluation.

1. Introduction to the Process

Figure 5.2 is the introduction sheet to the differentiation goal packet that teachers receive. It states the district's differentiation goal: *All Oakwood teachers will assess student readiness, interests, and strengths to regularly differentiate content, process, and product.* The introduction sheet also outlines the steps that teachers follow to write their differentiation goal: (a) self-assess using the nonevaluative Differentiation Rubric (Figure 5.3) to identify an aspect of differentiation as the goal; (b) use the Differentiation Choice Board (Figure 5.4) to select a professional development strategy, a collaboration strategy, and a visitation plan for their action plan; (c) select a sharing out strategy.

FIGURE 5.2

> ### *Phase I & II Differentiation Professional Goal Planning*
>
> This packet is designed to help you develop a professional goal related to our district's differentiation goal:
>
> *All Oakwood teachers will assess student readiness, interests, and strengths to regularly differentiate content, process, and product.*
>
> Here are the recommended steps for developing a professional goal aligned to our district's differentiation goal:
>
> 1. Use the Differentiation Rubric on the following page to self-assess where you are with differentiation and to give you an idea of what you want to focus on. ***This rubric is nonevaluative.*** Its purposes are to identify what differentiation is and to help you self-assess.
> 2. Use the Differentiation Choice Board on the next page to select an ongoing professional development strategy, a collaboration strategy, and a visitation plan as your Phase I & II Professional Performance Plan "action plan."
> 3. Use the Choice Board to select a "sharing out" strategy as the Method of Evaluation for your Phase I & II Professional Performance Plan.

In order to walk the reader through this process, we have invented Mara, a seventh-grade math teacher, as an example.

2. Differentiation Rubric: Identifying a Goal

Figure 5.3 is the two-page self-assessment rubric (written by the CORE Team) used by teachers to identify their relative strengths and weaknesses within differentiation. We encourage teachers to use a highlighter to mark statements on the rubric that reflect their current practice. Visually, then, teachers can quickly identify which domains of differentiation—differentiating for interest, readiness, and strength (learning profile) and differentiating through content, process, and product—are their strong points (Distinguished, Developing) and which need improvement (Basic). Ideally, teachers select a Basic or Developing area as the focus for their differentiation goal.

For example, within the past year Mara has begun to pretest before some major units of instruction and has therefore highlighted the statement "sometimes uses pretesting to inform instruction" in the Developing column for "differentiating for READINESS." During the past year, Mara experienced the benefits of pretesting. She learned from student data that she could skip teaching some skills and concepts altogether because her students had already mastered them. Other times she realized that she needed to backtrack to teach some missing prerequisite skills before teaching her grade level objectives. Additionally, some of her students were ready for extension and enrichment work. Since the pretesting she did seemed to increase her instructional acuity and efficiency, she decides that she wants to focus on moving up to the Distinguished column for READINESS: "Consistently uses pretesting to diagnose student readiness and inform instruction." She therefore writes "Consistently use pretesting prior to each new math unit" in the "Performance Goal" column on her Professional Performance Plan (Figure 5.5).

3. Differentiation Choice Board: Developing an Action Plan and Method of Evaluation

Research and experience tell us that to best serve student learning, teachers must engage in ongoing professional development, collaborate with their colleagues, and move beyond the isolation of their own classroom. The purpose of the Differentiation Choice Board, shown in Figure 5.4, is to provide teachers with a variety of choices through which they can attain each of these. The choice board requires teachers to select some type of ongoing professional development relevant to their goal, meeting the requirements of the federal No Child Left Behind Act's High Quality Professional Development mandate; to collaborate with a colleague (work with a specialist); and to visit another professional (get out of their classroom). It also lists the options for evaluation.

This choice board itself is a differentiation strategy. Indeed, choice boards are common, simple tools for differentiating learning processes. Our very use of this choice board is modeling differentiation. Our choice board is a way for educators to select options that are most meaningful to them while still meeting the nonnegotiable objectives of lifelong learning, using specialists' knowledge, and visiting other professionals. The last choice in each column is "Other." Teachers can always come up with another option that fits the purpose of the column.

After writing her differentiation goal, Mara uses the Differentiation Choice Board to write some of the action steps that she will take to meet her goal. She must select at least one option from each of the Action Plan columns (Ongoing PD, Collaboration, and Visitation) to include in her Professional Performance Plan (Figure 5.5). She decides to participate in a PLC focused on assessment practices (Ongoing PD), to collaborate with another seventh-grade math teacher named Dolores to develop pretests for each math unit

FIGURE 5.3 Differentiation Rubric

Domain		*Distinguished*
differentiating for...	*Interest*	<ul><li>assesses student interests (e.g., interest inventory) and uses to inform instruction</li><li>consistently offers students choices for learning</li><li>promotes student interests beyond the classroom</li><li>makes connections between content and student interests</li><li>connects most content to real-world experiences and situations</li><li>consistently plans instruction around student interests</li><li>consistently uses flexible grouping based on student interests</li></ul>
	Readiness	<ul><li>consistently uses pretesting to diagnose student readiness and inform instruction</li><li>consistently modifies curriculum for student readiness</li><li>consistently uses flexible grouping</li><li>uses ongoing assessment data to offer intervention and enrichment/extension as needed</li></ul>
	Strength (Learning Profile)	<ul><li>consistently teaches to multiple learning modalities (visual, auditory, tactile)</li><li>consistently integrates students' multiple intelligences into instruction over time (e.g. intrapersonal, interpersonal, logical/mathematic, verbal/linguistic, visual/spatial, bodily/kinesthetic, musical/rhythmic)</li><li>focuses and builds on student strengths</li></ul>

Developing	*Basic*
♦ has awareness of student interests ♦ sometimes offers students choices for learning ♦ develops student interests in the content area ♦ sometimes makes connections between content and student interests ♦ connects some content to real-world experiences and situations ♦ sometimes plans instruction around student interests ♦ sometimes uses flexible grouping based on student interests	♦ lacks awareness of student interests ♦ offers no choice for learning ♦ expects students to be interested in content ♦ makes no connections between content and student interests ♦ makes no connections between content and real world ♦ does not plan instruction around student interests ♦ does not use flexible grouping based on student interests
♦ sometimes uses pretesting to inform instruction ♦ sometimes modifies curriculum for student readiness ♦ sometimes uses flexible grouping ♦ does some intervention and enrichment/extension	♦ expects all students to have prerequisite skills (does not use pretesting to inform instruction) ♦ teaches to "the middle" (does not modify curriculum for student readiness) ♦ does not use flexible grouping; groups by "ability" ♦ fails significant numbers of students
♦ has awareness of student learning modalities ♦ sometimes considers multiple intelligences when planning instruction ♦ sometimes builds on student strengths	♦ lacks awareness of student learning modalities ♦ plans instruction without considering students' multiple intelligences ♦ focuses on student weaknesses

FIGURE 5.3 Differentiation Rubric *(continued)*

	Domain	Distinguished
differentiating through...	*Content*	♦ adjusts content based on all students' needs to meet standards ♦ varies teaching and stretches content every year ♦ provides intervention and enrichment as needed
	Process	♦ consistently uses multiple methods of grouping students ♦ uses a variety of instructional practices (cooperative learning, direct instruction, project-based learning, inquiry, questioning, etc.) ♦ adjusts rate of instruction and reteaches as needed ♦ provides students multiple and varied opportunities to practice skills (e.g., in class and homework)
	Product	♦ consistently uses a combination of formative and summative assessment ♦ consistently uses a combination of informal and formal assessments ♦ uses a variety of assessment strategies (pencil/paper tests, performance assessment, etc.) ♦ bases student evaluation on standards ♦ consistently provides students multiple opportunities to show what they know and provides students some choice ♦ consistently allows/provides re-assessments to promote student mastery

Developing	*Basic*
♦ adjusts content based on some students' needs to meet standards ♦ varies teaching slightly from year to year ♦ provides some intervention and enrichment	♦ does not adjust content based on students' needs ♦ teaches virtually the same way every year (the content does not change even though the students do) ♦ does not provide intervention and enrichment
♦ sometimes uses different methods of grouping students ♦ varies instructional practices at times ♦ adjusts rate of instruction and reteaches at times ♦ provides students some opportunities to practice skills	♦ primarily groups students homogeneously by "ability" (uses only one method of grouping students) ♦ primarily relies on lecture/direct instruction (does not vary instructional practices) ♦ does not adjust rate of instruction and/or reteach ♦ provides primarily skill and drill homework for practicing skills
♦ uses more summative than formative assessment ♦ sometimes uses a combination of informal and formal assessments ♦ sometimes varies assessment strategies ♦ bases student evaluation on standards and other criteria (e.g., effort or conduct) ♦ sometimes provides students multiple opportunities to show what they know ♦ sometimes allows/provides re-assessments to promote student mastery	♦ uses summative assessment exclusively ♦ uses formal or informal assessments exclusively ♦ uses one assessment strategy (e.g., pencil/paper tests) ♦ bases student evaluation largely on criteria other than standards (effort, neatness, conduct, etc.) and does not clearly tie evaluation to standards ♦ uses primarily one form of assessment (pencil/paper tests) ♦ tests for concepts and skills one time (does not allow/provide continual assessment)

68 ♦ Differentiation Is an Expectation

FIGURE 5.4 Differentiation Choice Board
This choice board is designed to help you complete your Phase I & II Professional Performance Plan form.

Action Plan (select at least one from each column)		
Ongoing PD (be a lifelong learner)	*Collaboration* (work with a specialist)	*Visitation* (get out of your classroom)
PLC	Reading specialist	Peer coaching*
University course	Intervention specialist	Intraschool observation*
Sequence of 4 Pizza & PD sessions (date/topics will be announced by PDC on September 15)	Media specialist	Interschool observation*
	TES (Gifted specialist)	Interdistrict observation*
Independent or group study or project	Counselor	Co-teaching*
Value Added Learning Network (online course)	Mentor/mentee	Modeling (teach for another teacher)
Action Research	Grade level team	Webcam/video
Independent book study	Department	Teacher walk-throughs
Javits Gifted Training	Interschool collaboration (e.g., 6th-grade math with 7th-grade math)	PD Day field visit
Online course (e.g., through Ed Impact)	Cross-grade/department collaboration	
Apply for National Board Certification		
Participation in National Board "Take One" Program		
OTHER	OTHER	OTHER

*Can use floating sub in Feb.

Method of Evaluation (select at least one)
Sharing Out (learn from each other)
Create video clip
Show-and-tell at faculty meeting
Lead a PD day session or participate in a sharing session
Present at a state, regional, or national conference
Handouts (work samples, assignments, assessments) distributed to colleagues or posted on your website and linked from CIA page
Write article for *OhioASCD Journal* or another professional journal
Lead Pizza & PD Session
Show-and-tell at grade-level or departmental meeting
Present/publish Action Research findings (on your website with link from CIA page, at a faculty meeting, at a PD day session, etc.)
Curricular Showcase at Board Meeting
Share assessment results of differentiated project or assignment with supervisor
Survey students specific to your goal topic and share results with your supervisor
Create a podcast
OTHER

(Collaboration), and to visit with an eighth-grade teacher to learn how he uses pretest data to form flexible math groups (Visitation). Mara writes these strategies in the Action Plan portion of her Professional Performance Plan.

Then Mara selects from the choice board a way to share what she has learned with her peers. She decides to do a show-and-tell with Dolores at a departmental meeting. She writes this in the Method of Evaluation column on her Professional Performance Plan.

4. Professional Performance Plan: Putting It All Together

Figure 5.5 is the document on which teachers write their differentiation goal, action plan, and method of evaluation. In the "Domain: Component" column, Mara notes which domain of Charlotte Danielson's *Enhancing Professional Practice: A Framework for Teaching* is applicable to her goal. She marks 1.C (Setting Instructional Outcomes) and 1.F (Designing Student Assessments). As already discussed, Mara writes "Consistently use pretesting prior to each new math unit" in the Performance Goal column. In the Action Plan column, as already discussed, she includes her participation in the assessment PLC, her collaboration with Dolores, and her visit with her eighth-grade colleague. There may be other steps to her action plan as well, such as how she will chart the data she gleans from pretests. Finally, in the Method of Evaluation column, she notes that she and Dolores will do a show-and-tell at their April department meeting and that she will share the same information with her supervisor during her end-of-year conference.

5. Conferencing and Summative Assessment

Early in the fall semester, all teachers meet with their supervisors to go over their goals chart. While some teachers come to this goals conference with general ideas and work with their supervisor to mold their ideas into a final document, other teachers come with a polished Professional Performance Plan that they go over with their principal. Principals must approve the plan and offer support to complete the plan, such as release time for the teacher's professional visit to another teacher.

Throughout the year, Mara works on her goal. Then, at a department meeting in April, Mara and Dolores do their show-and-tell, explaining how they select content for their pretests, administer and score the tests, and chart the data. They also describe the instructional decisions that they make based on the data and how the pretests have helped them better serve their whole class as well as individual students.

Mara shares this same information with her supervisor during her end-of-year goals conference, presenting her examples of pretests, data charts, instructional decisions, and benefits for students (e.g., revised instructional

FIGURE 5.5

Phase I & II Professional Performance Plan

Name: _____ School: _____ Grade/Subject: _____

Evaluator's Name: _____ School Year: _____ Date: _____

Domain: Component	Performance Goal	Action Plan	Method of Evaluation

Domain and component to be selected from *Enhancing Professional Practice: A Framework for Teaching* by Charlotte Danielson calendar, higher semester exam grades). Her supervisor uses this evidence to write up Mara's final evaluation for the year: Teachers' annual written evaluations specifically include summative assessment about the teachers' attainment of their differentiation goals.

Inside Oakwood

Below is an example of part of an elementary music teacher's Professional Performance Plan and his supervisor's summative assessment of that goal.

Performance Goal	*Action Plan*	*Method of Evaluation*
Differentiate music theory lessons to meet needs of students.	Use technology to collect data to help determine students' needs and assess progress. Empower students to work at own level. Use student musicians when appropriate for school events. Utilize skill-based and interest-based centers for low participation students. Use a variety of teaching methods to meet needs of all students.	Sharing programs and other school-wide events where music is utilized. Podcasts by students and classes. Parents, staff, and student surveys. Work samples.

Mr. Thompson was pleased with his work toward the goals, which he successfully addressed. His focus was music theory, creating lessons to meet the various student needs. He shared many strategies to differentiate instruction for his general music classes. He collaborated with the band director and often sat in on fifth-grade band sessions to better understand instrumental student levels. Centers were used including technology (websites, student clickers, keyboard). Students practiced notation, range, tempo, etc., and created melodies to be published. Student publications and musicians were used during programs. In addition to attending and leading professional development days and working with his team on waiver days, he completed coursework and met with the band director to increase music theory knowledge. He collaborated with staff at Smith and Harman Elementary Schools. Student surveys reflected a safe environment . . .

6. Support Offered to Teachers

Based on the above paragraphs, this process may seem complex and confusing. There are several support mechanisms in place to help teachers make their way through this process:

- *Segment at a faculty meeting*: At a faculty meeting at the beginning of the year, the principal distributes the differentiation goal packet (Figures 5.2–5.5) and reviews the expectation that all teachers write at least one professional differentiation goal. Then the building's CORE Team members walk their faculty through the process using a multimedia presentation and one of themselves as an example.
- *Video podcast*: Using a software program called Screenflow, we have created a video podcast that walks the viewer step-by-step through the process. The podcast resides on the district's website and can be viewed by teachers as many times as they wish. (To view the podcast, go to www.oakwood.k12.oh.us and click on the Director of Curriculum link.)
- *Pizza & PD session*: Each building's CORE Team members hold a Pizza & PD session after school in September. The purpose of the session is that all attendees leave the session with their professional goal completely written. These Pizza & PD sessions are among our most popular. Teachers appreciate having help as they write their goal, and they like being able to discuss their ideas with other participants in the sessions. Such conversations have led to some interesting collaboration and visitation plans. For example, a kindergarten teacher connected with an elementary media specialist who helped her pick out some science picture books to use with her advanced students.

By aligning teacher evaluation to differentiation and by requiring teachers not only to differentiate but to intentionally grow in differentiation in a targeted, focused way, Oakwood's professional differentiation goals have become our most effective fire strategy.

"Required Choice" Professional Development

In Oakwood, all teachers must participate in three types of professional development:

1. They are obligated to attend our district's two professional development days. As discussed in the previous chapter, teachers can choose

from a variety of concurrent sessions or attend a field visit. They self-select options to differentiate for their needs and interests.
2. By contract, teachers must complete seven hours of self-selected professional development during noncontract time. This can include Pizza & PD sessions, PLCs, Centerville Summer and Winter Institutes, university coursework, and so on (see Chapter 4 for more information on these options). Within this requirement, teachers choose what type of professional development to pursue. Teachers get their principal's approval for their specific activities prior to completing them. Most Oakwood teachers earn far beyond seven hours of noncontract professional development time each year.
3. As discussed in the preceding section, our teacher evaluation program requires teachers to complete some type of ongoing professional development related to their differentiation goal.

Through these three avenues, teachers must complete at least 21 hours of professional development per year. Within this requirement, however, they have a great deal of choice so that they can customize their professional development according to their readiness, interests, and learning styles. Again, this is a way to hold teachers accountable for growing in their ability to differentiate while simultaneously modeling differentiation.

The Toxic 2

According to Reeves, when schools initiate major changes, about 17% of teachers are change leaders, 53% implement the change and are willing to model it, 28% are fence-sitters who are aware of the change initiative but have not implemented it, and the final "toxic" 2% are "either defiantly unaware of leadership expectations or, more likely, actively opposed" to them (2009, p. 53).

The point here is that while deep and widespread implementation of a change initiative is absolutely necessary for significant growth in student achievement, the "Toxic 2" will always defy, undermine, or ignore the change. Reeves recommends being realistic in how you invest your time, energy, and resources: "The evidence suggests that leaders are better advised to lavish their time, appreciation, and support on 70% of the faculty—the 17 percent who are leaders and the 53 percent who are models—rather than continue to engage in ineffective and emotionally draining combat with the Toxic 2" (Reeves, 2009, p. 54).

While we completely agree with Reeves' writings on the Toxic 2—and we could name a couple of people in that category—we have learned that what might look like the makings of a Toxic 2-er could actually be an educator about to metamorphose into a teacher leader.

If we were betting people, we might have wagered that Rob Guizzo, the 35-year veteran science teacher introduced in Chapter 4, would be a candidate for Toxic 2 status. From the outset, he—by his own admission—ranted and railed against differentiation in general and the fact that he was mandated to do it (fire strategies) in particular. Yet through his participation in PLCs—his choice for ongoing professional development for his professional differentiation goal—he found the collegial support and acceptance that he needed to try differentiation while maintaining his ontological security and sense of self as a teacher. What he learned from his colleagues provided him with vetted strategies and ideas that he could incorporate into his instruction without feeling as though he was jettisoning all he knew and had done before. We are still in awe of the transformation that he has made, and we respect the risks that he has taken. We further appreciate his willingness to share with other colleagues through the Pizza & PD session that he co-facilitated with a colleague—his form of sharing-out for his differentiation goal. Rob has taught us not to make assumptions about who will be a Toxic 2-er and that it is a good thing that we are not betting people.

Summary

Reeves debunked as myth the adage that "just a little bit better is good enough." Because meaningful improvement in student learning requires widespread adoption of a change initiative, fire strategies are needed to push educators toward change. The first fire strategy presented in this chapter is to differentiate supervision based on teacher need and according to a continuum that ranges from directive through collaborative to nondirective supervision. The second—and most powerful—strategy is to evaluate teachers' use of differentiation through differentiated teacher evaluation practices. The third strategy is required-choice professional development. Regardless of the passion with which light and fire strategies are applied, Reeves's research suggests that there will likely be a "Toxic 2" percent of teachers who evade—or attempt to undermine—change. This reality should not be allowed to derail change for differentiation. Likewise, leaders must take care to recognize not only that a Toxic 2-er may be able to change, but also the Toxic 2-er may become a teacher leader.

References

Danielson, C. (2007). *Enhancing professional practice: A framework for teaching.* 2nd ed. Alexandria, VA: ASCD.

Glickman, C., Gordon, S., and Ross-Gordon, J. (2001). *SuperVision and instructional leadership.* 5th ed. Boston: Allyn & Bacon.

Reeves, D. (2009). *Leading change in your school: How to conquer myths, build commitment, and get results.* Alexandria, VA: ASCD.

Starratt, R. J. (1993). *The drama of leadership.* London: Falmer Press.

6

Assessment, Instruction, Materials, and Technology: Tools to Support Differentiation

> ***This chapter will***
>
> 1. illustrate the importance of assessment in the differentiated school or district (pretesting, assessing for learning modalities and multiple intelligences, etc.)
> 2. identify instructional approaches that are conducive to differentiation
> 3. identify the importance of instructional materials and technology that support differentiation
> 4. discuss differentiated programming (services for special populations)

"Differentiation is at the foremost of my thoughts as I plan my instruction and while I am in the process of instructing. I do not plan any activities or assessments without first thinking of differentiation."
—Lori Morris, Oakwood High School English teacher

This chapter is really about the *c* word—*curriculum*. When we use the word *curriculum*, we are referring to what is taught, how it is taught (general instructional and pedagogical approaches), how it is assessed, and what instructional materials (technology and print) are used. Some administrators may feel more comfortable with the concepts of communication and hiring and less comfortable with curricular matters. While this chapter might be uncomfortable, give it a chance. A curriculum oriented toward differentiation will go a long way in making differentiation a reality in every classroom.

We believe that in order for differentiation to become part of a school's lifeblood and culture, it needs to be central to all conversations and decisions regarding assessment, instruction, materials, and technology. Differentiation cannot be viewed as something that administrators hope will happen behind the closed doors of individual classrooms. If school and district leaders want differentiation to become part of every classroom, it needs to be planned for and implemented through systemic approaches to assessment, instruction, materials, and technology. In other words, leading conversations and decisions about these topics is a crucial part of the building and district leader's role. This chapter, therefore, focuses on how building and district leaders can think about the assessment practices, instructional approaches and materials, and technology that will best support systemic differentiation. This chapter is *not* an exhaustive discussion of all realms of differentiated curriculum. Rather, this chapter is meant to get the reader thinking in the direction of curriculum to support differentiation.

Assessment: The Linchpin of the Differentiated Classroom

In a differentiated school, assessment cannot be reduced to a chapter or unit test given at the end of instruction. Instead, differentiation requires assessing for learning strengths and interests (e.g., modalities, multiple intelligences, and interest inventories), as well as student readiness (often in the form of pretesting). Additionally, teachers in differentiated classrooms regularly use formative assessment to gauge student learning and inform ongoing instruction and reteaching.

Preassessment

Before planning instruction, teachers who differentiate need to know who their students are as learners and what levels of skills and understanding they have. There are three main types of preassessments that teachers who differentiate use:

1. *Interest inventory*: This is a way to get to know what students are like as people and as learners. It can provide insight into what motivates them and intrigues them. This information can be used to develop lessons that are richly meaningful and engaging for students.
A quick Google search for "student interest inventory" will provide a wealth of sample interest inventories that educators can modify for their own purposes. Figure 6.1 shows a differentiated activity used by Bridget Fiore, a social studies teacher at Oakwood Junior High School, that helps her get to know her students.
2. *Learning profile*: According to Carol Ann Tomlinson (March, 2010a), a student's learning profile consists of, among other factors, intelligence preferences and learning styles:
    a. Intelligence preferences (e.g., Gardner's multiple intelligence theory and Sternberg's triarchic theory of intelligence) are neurologically based and hard-wired in the brain. They therefore tend to remain stable over time. Teachers can leverage students' intelligence preferences to motivate (differentiation by interest), to link new learning to prior knowledge (differentiation by readiness), and to provide students with choices about how to show what they know (differentiated products).
    b. Learning style is composed of numerous tendencies, including learning modalities (visual, spatial, and kinesthetic), and preferences such as working independently or collaboratively, sitting at a desk versus reclining on a sofa, and working in bright light or soft light. Learning style preferences tend to shift with circumstances, such as students' familiarity with the topic, whether the content area is a strength for the student, the student's level of stress—even the time of day. Teachers thus must understand that students' learning styles will present differently over time. To best serve students' variable learning styles, teachers can "provide options for students, help them make choices and evaluate the choices, and guide them in determining what is working for them at a given time" (Tomlinson, 2010b). The keys here are choice, flexibility, and openness.

FIGURE 6.1 Interest Inventory

Name _____ # _____

What's your HISTORY?

Directions: I want to get to know you ASAP! Using words and pictures, tell me your HISTORY, including what you like to read, eat, write, listen to, study, and play, and also what you don't like to read, eat, study, write, or play. Tell me about your family, where you live, where you've lived before, and for sure tell me as much as you can about what's UNIQUE about you. Also, tell me about the kinds of things that help you learn. And tell me your thoughts about learning American history, too. The more you tell me about yourself, the better I get to know you.

To earn your best score, you must
- Write about yourself.
- Draw about yourself.
- Include your history.
- Include your thoughts on studying American history.
- Include something UNIQUE about yourself.
- Include information about how you learn.
- Include some of your outside-of-school interests such as reading or sports.
- Include info about your family .
- Proofread your work!

You can write and draw in the blank space below and on back, or you can write on notebook paper. As long as you can check all the boxes above, there's no certain length or limit. Turn in this sheet along with your writing. I can't wait to get to know you a bit better.

Inside Oakwood

What follows is an example of how Oakwood Junior High, which serves about 350 seventh and eighth graders, is collecting and disseminating learner profile information.

At Oakwood Junior High School, CORE Team member (see Chapter 2 for information about Oakwood's CORE Team) and gifted intervention specialist Amanda Ammer surveys each incoming seventh-grade class to get a sense of students' learning modalities and multiple intelligences (MIs). She uses an instrument that she developed (see Figure 6.2) from a variety of

FIGURE 6.2 Learning Styles and Multiple Intelligences Survey

1. After I write a letter, I ask someone to read it aloud to me so that I know how it sounds.
   a. True
   b. False

2. I learn better if someone reads a book to me than if I read silently to myself.
   a. True
   b. False

3. I understand more from talking about a subject in class than from reading about it.
   a. True
   b. False

4. I understand the news better if I hear it on the radio rather than read it in the newspaper.
   a. True
   b. False

5. Saying the multiplication tables over and over again would help me remember them better than writing them over and over.
   a. True
   b. False

6. I enjoy discussing questions about life and its meaning.
   a. True
   b. False

7. I enjoy reading ancient and modern philosophers.
   a. True
   b. False

8. It is important for me to see my role in the "big picture" of things.
   a. True
   b. False

FIGURE 6.2 Learning Styles and Multiple Intelligences Survey *(continued)*

9. Relaxation and meditation are rewarding to me.
    a. True
    b. False

10. Studying history, culture, and art gives me perspective on life.
    a. True
    b. False

11. I am a team player.
    a. True
    b. False

12. I dislike working alone.
    a. True
    b. False

13. I learn best when I interact with others.
    a. True
    b. False

14. I pay attention to social issues and causes.
    a. True
    b. False

15. Study groups are very helpful to me.
    a. True
    b. False

16. For me, working alone can be just as productive as working in a group.
    a. True
    b. False

17. I am strongly aware of my moral beliefs.
    a. True
    b. False

18. I like to be involved in causes that help others.
    a. True
    b. False

19. My attitude affects how I learn.
    a. True
    b. False

20. Social justice issues concern me.
    a. True
    b. False

21. I enjoy making things with my hands.
    a. True
    b. False

22. I learn by doing.
    a. True
    b. False

23. I like working with tools.
    a. True
    b. False

24. I prefer classes in which I am moving around and doing things.
    a. True
    b. False

FIGURE 6.2 Learning Styles and Multiple Intelligences Survey *(continued)*

25. I pick up new dance steps or athletic plays quickly and easily.
    a. True
    b. False

26. I get easily frustrated with disorganized people.
    a. True
    b. False

27. I keep things neat and orderly.
    a. True
    b. False

28. Reasoning puzzles are fun for me.
    a. True
    b. False

29. Step-by-step instructions are a big help to me.
    a. True
    b. False

30. Structure helps me to be successful.
    a. True
    b. False

31. I enjoy making many kinds of music.
    a. True
    b. False

32. I pick up on patterns easily.
    a. True
    b. False

33. I've always been interested in playing an instrument.
    a. True
    b. False

34. Moving to the beat is easy for me.
    a. True
    b. False

35. Remembering song lyrics is easy for me.
    a. True
    b. False

36. Animals are important in my life.
    a. True
    b. False

37. Hiking and camping are enjoyable for me.
    a. True
    b. False

38. I enjoy studying biology, botany, and/or zoology.
    a. True
    b. False

39. I enjoy working in a garden.
    a. True
    b. False

40. Putting things in order makes sense to me.
    a. True
    b. False

FIGURE 6.2 Learning Styles and Multiple Intelligences Survey *(continued)*

41. Debates and public speaking are activities I like to do.
    a. True
    b. False

42. I write for pleasure.
    a. True
    b. False

43. I enjoy reading all kinds of materials.
    a. True
    b. False

44. It is easy for me to explain my ideas to others.
    a. True
    b. False

45. Taking notes helps me remember and understand.
    a. True
    b. False

46. I am good at reading maps.
    a. True
    b. False

47. I like to draw pictures to remember things.
    a. True
    b. False

48. I remember information best when I use a graphic organizer or a web.
    a. True
    b. False

49. Three-dimensional puzzles are fun for me.
    a. True
    b. False

50. I can recall things in mental pictures in my head.
    a. True
    b. False

noncopyrighted sources, keeping it brief and using student-friendly language to get at which MIs and learning modalities best reflect students' intelligence preferences and learning styles (while recognizing that learning styles are variable over time). Students respond to the instrument on a Scantron form. Ammer then collects and analyzes the data. She documents the information in an Excel spreadsheet that lists each student's name and the student's primary learning modality and MI. To each teacher she sends a copy of the Excel file as well as a document describing the modalities and intelligences and what types of assignments and learning activities are best aligned to each (see Figures 6.3 and 6.4). She also provides this same information to each student, using a highlighter to mark the student's primary modality and MI.

A word of caution: Assigning particular students particular tasks based on intelligence preferences and learning styles is unwise. To do so would require that the instrument being used to identify intelligence preferences has been deemed statistically valid and reliable and that learning styles are stable over time. As neither is the case, this information should be considered suggestive and tentative. The tool should not be used to categorize students but rather to get a general sense of the diversity within the student body and within any given class.

When our teachers reviewed this data, they were surprised at how many students—on this particular inventory at this particular time—leaned toward the tactile and kinesthetic. While recognizing that learning styles shift with circumstances, teachers reflected on ways in which they could integrate options for students to engage in meaningful tactile and kinesthetic learning activities.

Yes, this process takes a great deal of time and hard work. However, the benefits are many. Because students' intelligence preferences do not change radically within 24 months, teachers can use the multiple intelligence data for students in both seventh and eighth grades. Teachers can reflect on the data as a whole faculty as well as individually and can use the information to inform building-level decisions (e.g., which exploratory classes provide the best opportunities for visual and spatial learners) as well as classroom-level decisions (how to introduce, reinforce, or reteach content). This information also empowers students by making them more aware of—and responsible for—their own learning. Finally, doing this activity building-wide communicates to the faculty and students that this information is important and should be used to inform differentiated instruction.

♦ ♦ ♦ ♦ ♦ ♦ ♦ ♦ ♦

3. *Readiness preassessment*: This type of preassessment is usually administered just prior to a new unit of instruction. Readiness preassessments cover the important prerequisite knowledge and skills students need to have in order to be successful with the new material as well as the key skills and concepts that will be taught in the upcoming unit of instruction. Readiness preassessments can show teachers
    ♦ *what students already know*: Teachers can therefore avoid the redundancy of unwittingly reteaching secure skills and concepts.
    ♦ *what prerequisite skills and concepts students do not have and will need to be taught before they can learn the current objectives*: Sometimes teachers need to go back and teach certain bridge skills and concepts to link what students already know to what they need to learn. Without attention to necessary bridge skills and concepts, a teacher's instruction on current concepts is fruitless.

FIGURE 6.3

Last Name	First Name	Learning style
Anderson	Diane	Kinesthetic
Atkins	Albert	Kinesthetic
Baker	Deborah	Kinesthetic
Barboza	Christine	Kinesthetic Visual
Chagares	John	Kinesthetic
Doyno	Ruth	Kinesthetic
Giles	Kenneth	Kinesthetic
Hoffman	Kenneth	Kinesthetic
Issenberg	Helen	Kinesthetic
Korn	David	Kinesthetic
Larsen	Tom	Kinesthetic
Mahoney	Patricia	Auditory Kinesthetic Visual
Nagin	Theodore	Auditory Kinesthetic Visual
Padgett	Nathaniel	Kinesthetic
Parker	Kim	Kinesthetic
Qunn	William	Auditory Kinesthetic Visual
Rainaldi	Thomas	Kinesthetic
Reynolds	Jennifer	Kinesthetic
Sann	Jonathan	Kinesthetic
Schuman	Elizabeth	Kinesthetic
Sobell	Roger	Kinesthetic
Toll	Peter	Kinesthetic Visual
Tucker	Virginia	Kinesthetic
Ungar	Bruce	Kinesthetic
Viccaro	Mary	Kinesthetic
Vidler	Matthew	Auditory Kinesthetic
Wachs	Joseph	Auditory Kinesthetic
Warren	Rebecca	Kinesthetic
Zimmerman	Nancy	Kinesthetic
Zook	Jason	Auditory Kinesthetic Visual

Intelligences
Musical
Interpersonal Kinesthetic Logical Musical
Interpersonal Kinesthetic Musical
Kinesthetic Logical Musical Naturalist Visual
Intrapersonal Kinesthetic
Kinesthetic Logical Musical
Existential Intrapersonal Kinesthetic Naturalist
Intrapersonal Kinesthetic Logical Musical Naturalist
Interpersonal Kinesthetic
Interpersonal Intrapersonal Kinesthetic Naturalist Verbal
Kinesthetic Logical
Existential Interpersonal Intrapersonal Kinesthetic Musical Naturalist Verbal Visual
Existential Interpersonal Intrapersonal Kinesthetic Musical Naturalist Verbal Visual
Existential Interpersonal Kinesthetic Musical
Existential Interpersonal Intrapersonal Kinesthetic Logical Musical Naturalist Verbal
Interpersonal Kinesthetic Musical Naturalist Visual
Interpersonal Kinesthetic Musical Naturalist Verbal
Kinesthetic Musical
Kinesthetic Logical
Interpersonal Kinesthetic Musical
Kinesthetic
Existential Interpersonal Intrapersonal Kinesthetic Musical Verbal Visual
Existential Logical
Existential Intrapersonal Kinesthetic Musical Naturalist
Interpersonal Kinesthetic Logical Naturalist
Existential Interpersonal Kinesthetic Logical Musical
Kinesthetic
Existential Interpersonal Kinesthetic Logical Naturalist
Existential Logical Musical Verbal
Interpersonal Kinesthetic Logical Musical Visual

FIGURE 6.4 How Students Learn

Learning Styles *(how people learn)*	*Multiple Intelligences* *(how people show what they've learned)*
Visual learners learn mainly through seeing things. They learn best when they can see a picture in their minds. If they see something, such as printed directions, pictures, lists, or maps, they can understand it better. They comprehend better when they read a book than when they hear someone read it to them. **Auditory learners** learn mainly through hearing. They learn best by listening and responding verbally. They can tell you the answer even though they have only been listening. **Kinesthetic learners** learn through their bodies. They learn best by handling, touching, and manipulating things. They are movement-oriented; when they have to sit still, their bodies seem to "go to sleep." One way to involve them is to have them write their thoughts down.	**Existential intelligence** shows a sensitivity and capacity to tackle deep questions about human existence, such as the meaning of life, why we die, and how we got here. **Interpersonal intelligence** shows a capacity to detect and respond appropriately to the moods, motivations, and desires of others. **Intrapersonal intelligence** shows a capacity to be self-aware and in tune with inner feelings, values, beliefs, and thinking processes. **Bodily/kinesthetic intelligence** shows an ability to control one's body movements and to handle objects skillfully. **Logical/mathematical intelligence** shows an ability to think conceptually and abstractly and to discern logical or numerical patterns. **Musical intelligence** shows an ability to produce and appreciate rhythm, pitch, and timbre. **Naturalist intelligence** shows an ability to recognize and categorize plants, animals, and other objects in nature. **Verbal/linguistic intelligence** shows well-developed verbal skills and sensitivity to the sounds, meanings, and rhythms of words. **Visual/spatial intelligence** shows a capacity to think in images and pictures and to visualize accurately.

FIGURE 6.4 How Students Learn *(continued)*

Learning Style Activities *(how people learn)*	*Multiple Intelligence Activities* *(how people show what they've learned)*
Visual Learners ♦ writing & note-taking ♦ written instruction ♦ interactive white boards ♦ painting, collages ♦ demonstrations ♦ reading assignments ♦ audiovisual materials ♦ quiet time to work alone **Auditory Learners** ♦ lectures ♦ verbal instruction ♦ student speeches ♦ audiotapes ♦ discussions, debates ♦ reading aloud ♦ music & sound effects ♦ storytelling **Kinesthetic Learners** ♦ hands-on activities ♦ labs, manipulatives ♦ foldables ♦ large-motor skill games ♦ sculpture, woodworking ♦ skits & plays ♦ dance & movement ♦ physical relaxation activities ♦ opportunities to move	**Existential Intelligence** ♦ participating in discussions ♦ describing big ideas ♦ answering reflective questions **Interpersonal Intelligence** ♦ solving real-life problems ♦ performing/producing cooperatively ♦ role-playing **Intrapersonal Intelligence** ♦ journaling ♦ writing editorials ♦ examining ethical issues **Bodily/Kinesthetic Intelligence** ♦ creating skits & plays ♦ using gestures & foldables ♦ building a model **Logical/Mathematical Intelligence** ♦ analyzing data via lab work ♦ testing hypotheses ♦ examining patterns with spreadsheets **Musical Intelligence** ♦ writing a song or poem ♦ interpreting music & patterns ♦ using music software **Naturalist Intelligence** ♦ categorizing plants & animals ♦ collecting artifacts ♦ recording changes over time **Verbal/Linguistic Intelligence** ♦ creating advertisements ♦ comparing & contrasting ♦ reading and evaluating nonfiction **Visual/Spatial Intelligence** ♦ creating graphic organizers ♦ designing artistic interpretations ♦ making & interpreting maps

- *which students need something different from what other students need*: Some students, for example, may already have mastery-level knowledge (80–85% accuracy) of material about to be taught. These students obviously need something different than what other students need. Teachers may elect to group these students together for extension or enrichment for the duration of the new unit of instruction. At Oakwood's two elementary schools, students are routinely preassessed prior to each new unit of math instruction. In grades 5 and 6, students who demonstrate mastery on preassessments participate in flexible groups taught by the gifted enrichment specialist.

Formative Assessment

W. James Popham (2008) defines formative assessment this way: "Formative assessment is a planned process in which teachers or students use assessment-based evidence to adjust what they're currently doing" (2008, p. 6). In a differentiated classroom, teachers assess students on an ongoing basis during an instructional unit to determine who understands the material, who does not, and who needs more challenge. Formative assessment strategies can include exit slips (students respond to a prompt regarding the day's learning objectives on a slip of paper that they hand to the teacher as they leave class), short, frequent quizzes, and use of student response systems, which will be discussed later in this chapter.

♦ ♦ ♦ ♦ ♦ ♦ ♦ ♦ ♦

Inside Oakwood

Brianna Doyal, an English and language arts teacher at Oakwood Junior High School, routinely has students respond to a question or prompt on an index card that they hand to her as they leave class. She reads through the cards immediately, before the next class begins, "filing" each of them into one of the grooves between her fingers based on whether the student's response shows secure understanding, some understanding, or need for reteaching. She uses this information, indicating which students need reteaching, retouching (following up briefly to hone understanding and correct any misperceptions), or enrichment and extension, to inform her ongoing lesson planning.

♦ ♦ ♦ ♦ ♦ ♦ ♦ ♦ ♦

The type of formative assessment done is less important than that the data gleaned from the assessment be used to inform differentiated instruction.

Differentiated Instructional Approaches

Some instructional approaches are differentiated by their very nature. Three of these are writing workshop, reading workshop, and inquiry-based instruction. While a thorough discussion of these approaches is beyond the scope of this chapter, the following description of each demonstrates how the approach itself is differentiated.

Writing Workshop

Different people have different notions of what writing workshop means and looks like. Generally, though, writing workshop includes self-selected, independent writing (genre, topic, and form of publishing selected by the student), regular student-teacher writing conferences, and mini-lessons for the whole class or a subsection of the class that are based on grade level standards and needs identified in student writing conferences.

Writing workshop is differentiated in a number of ways. First, it promotes choice (differentiation based on student interest) in a student's selection of genre, writing topic, and method of publishing (e.g., book for class library, online poetry anthology). Second, through the use of one-on-one writing conferences, the teacher coaches each student on the skills needed (e.g., organizing content logically, writing a powerful lead, using vivid verbs) to improve the student's writing. Third, through the use of ongoing monitoring of students' writing, the teacher can develop mini-lessons that are specific to the needs of the class—or a subsection of the class—at a given point in time, making instruction more targeted and responsive.

♦ ♦ ♦ ♦ ♦ ♦ ♦ ♦ ♦

Inside Oakwood

Oakwood fourth-grade teacher Monica Brouwer led a two-year PLC on writing workshop for elementary teachers. In addition to discussions on topics such as setting up and managing writing workshop, conducting writing conferences, and assessing and grading students' writing, the group also did some make-it, take-it sessions where they made management tools. For example, teachers used the sticker photos they receive each year from the school photographer to make photo magnets of students that students would move to the appropriate column on a magnetic chart board to indicate which writing workshop task they were doing that day (prewriting, drafting, revising, conferencing, editing, publishing). Additionally, the group "just shared ideas about writing." Monica says of writing workshop: "I love it, and it is the best form of teaching writing that I have ever used." The language arts teacher who had Monica's students the following year commented that their "enthusiasm for writing carried into the next year."

◆ ◆ ◆ ◆ ◆ ◆ ◆ ◆ ◆

For more information about writing workshop, see:

- Marybeth Alley and Barbara Orehovec. (2007). *Revisiting the writing workshop: Management, assessment, and mini-lessons.* New York: Scholastic Teaching Resources.
- M. Colleen Cruz and Lucy Calkins. (2008). *A quick guide to reaching struggling writers, K–5 (Workshop Help Desk).* Portsmouth, NH: Firsthand.
- Ralph Fletcher and JoAnn Portalupi. (2001). *Writing workshop: The essential guide.* Portsmouth, NH: Heinemann.
- Katie Wood Ray, with Lisa Cleaveland. (2004). *About the authors: Writing workshop with our youngest writers.* Portsmouth, NH: Heinemann.
- Katie Wood Ray and Lester L. Laminack. (2001). *The writing workshop: Working through the hard parts (and they're all hard parts).* Urbana, IL: NCTE.

Reading Workshop

Reading workshop is somewhat analogous to writing workshop. During a portion of reading workshop, students read self-selected content at their independent reading level. The teacher develops mini-lessons for the whole class or a subsection of the class on relevant reading skills (e.g., using context clues to identify the meaning of unknown words, drawing inferences, plot structure of fiction, cause and effect) and confers with students individually about their reading. Additionally, reading workshop often includes targeted, small-group instruction via guided reading groups or literature circles.

Like writing workshop, reading workshop promotes differentiation through choice of independent reading material (based on student interest and reading level), ongoing monitoring through individualized reading conferences, and mini-lessons that are specific to the identified needs of the class or a subsection of the class.

For more information about reading workshop, see:

- Kathy Collins. (2004). *Growing readers: Units of study in the primary classroom*. Portland, ME: Stenhouse.
- Ellin Oliver Keene and Susan Zimmermann. (2007). *Mosaic of thought: The power of comprehension strategy instruction*. 2nd ed. Portsmouth, NH: Heinemann.
- Frank Serafini. (2001). *The reading workshop: Creating space for readers*. Portsmouth, NH: Heinemann.

Inquiry

As educators, we often think of inquiry as something done in constructivist science classrooms. Actually, a broader definition of inquiry-based instruction is applicable across content areas. According to Alan Colburn (2000, p. 42), inquiry-based instruction is "the creation of a classroom where students are engaged in essentially open-ended, student-centered, hands-on activities." There are several approaches to inquiry, as articulated by Colburn:

- *Structured inquiry*. The teacher provides students with a hands-on problem to investigate, as well as the procedures and materials, but does not inform them of expected outcomes. Students are to discover relationships between variables or otherwise generalize from data collected. These types of investigations are similar to those known as cookbook activities, although a cookbook activity generally includes more direction than a structured inquiry activity about what students are to observe and which data they are to collect.
- *Guided inquiry*. The teacher provides only the materials and problem to investigate. Students devise their own procedure to solve the problem.
- *Open inquiry*. Students formulate their own problem to investigate. Open inquiry, in many ways, is analogous to doing science. Science fair activities are often examples of open inquiry.

Inquiry promotes differentiation by providing students with the opportunity to approach a problem, find a way to solve it, and report their results in ways that best fit their strengths and interests. Teachers can strategically group students (homogeneously or heterogeneously, based on readiness, modalities, multiple intelligences, or interests) or allow students to self-select groups (providing choice). Additionally, teachers can differentiate the level of support or scaffolding that they provide to various groups.

Inquiry-based approaches are not limited to the science classroom. Math investigations and problem-based social studies simulations are examples of inquiry-based approaches, as the next section illustrates.

For more information about inquiry-based instruction, see:

- James A. Minstrell and Emily H. van Zee, eds. (2000). *Inquiring into inquiry learning and teaching science*. Washington, DC: American Association for the Advancement of Science.
- Diane E. Newby and Peter L. Higgs. (2005). Using inquiry to teach social studies. *Charter Schools Resource Journal*, 6(1).
- Wendy Saul, Jeanne Reardon, Charles R. Pearce, Donna Dieckman, and Donna Neutze. (2002). *Science workshop: Reading, writing, and thinking like a scientist*. 2nd ed. Portsmouth, NH: Heinemann.

Math Investigations

One type of inquiry that is commonly used in reform[1] math curricula is investigations. Investigations usually center around a real-world situation or problem that requires students—often working collaboratively—to reason mathematically through the problem and use concepts and skills currently under study. The Connected Math Project (www.connectedmath.msu.edu/components/student.shtml) describes its investigations this way:

> An Investigation includes two to five carefully sequenced Problems. Each Problem is launched by the teacher; then the students explore the Problem individually, in groups, or as a whole class. As students solve the Problems, they uncover important mathematical relationships

---

1. By "reform" math we refer to approaches to math curriculum that emphasize conceptual understanding of math as well as mathematical reasoning, use of real-world, contextualized math problem-solving, collaborative learning, and communicating mathematically (graphically, verbally, in writing, numerically, symbolically, and through drawing or modeling).

and develop problem-solving strategies and skills. A summary occurs at the end of each Problem. The teacher pulls the class together and helps students explicitly describe the mathematics of the Problem, ideas, patterns, relationships, and strategies they found and used.

A reform math approach is used in grades K–12 in Oakwood, and instruction in grades 7 and up centers around math investigations conducted by students. The use of investigations promotes differentiation in several ways. First, teachers can elect to group students according to learning profile or readiness or can allow students to self-select groups. Strategic or choice grouping can be a useful differentiation strategy. Second, the nature of math investigations is such that students can take multiple pathways to solving the investigation. Thus, the very approaches that students take will be differentiated, and when these various approaches are shared with the entire class during a debriefing, all students benefit from seeing multiple pathways used. Third, teachers can provide different students or groups of students with different investigations to best fit their readiness level. Additionally, teachers can differentiate the amount and type of interaction and support they provide to the group, based on need.

Instructional Materials Aligned to Differentiation

There are three main ways in which instructional materials can support differentiation. Some materials are centered on a differentiated approach to instruction (as described above). Others include differentiation strategies in the teacher's edition (TE) or supplemental booklets. Other publishers provide leveled readers to accompany core textbooks. Each of these approaches is discussed below.

- ♦ *Differentiation as central approach to text*: Some instructional materials are designed around a pedagogy that promotes differentiation. As described above, math investigations, by their very nature, are conducive to differentiation. While math investigations can be used by anyone teaching math, some (usually reform) math textbooks and core materials center on investigations. For example, our district uses *Connected Math* and Key Curriculum Press's *Discovering* series, both of which use investigations as a primary instructional strategy. Some of our elementary social studies classrooms use TCI's *History Alive!* series, which is based on multiple intelligences theory and utilizes problem-solving activities and simulations. Our elementary classrooms all use Delta/Foss science inquiry kits as part of core instruction.

- *Differentiation strategies in TEs and supplemental booklets*: Almost all publishers now include some type of differentiation with their textbook sets. Sometimes this is in the form of suggested activities written into TEs for students who need enrichment and extension or additional support and scaffolding. Some publishers offer supplemental booklets filled with a variety of differentiation strategies, from graphic organizers to extension projects to additional worksheets. Let the buyer beware: These materials are not all created equal, and we recommend close scrutiny of publishers' differentiation materials. We have found that some are of a fairly high quality and others seem to be a low-quality afterthought on the part of publishers to assuage educators' clamoring for differentiation strategies.
- *Leveled readers that accompany core texts*: Many publishers of science and social studies textbooks offer leveled readers that support core texts. These usually short, full-color, glossy books are offered at three different reading levels: below grade level, on grade level, and above grade level. Similar to the aforementioned supplemental differentiation booklets offered by publishers, these readers range in quality from well-written, engaging ways to meet the needs of students to daft, ill-written regurgitations of the textbook material. It is incumbent upon educators to evaluate the quality of these readers carefully and not to assume that because they are leveled they will serve the differentiated classroom well.

Technology to Support the Differentiated Classroom

There are innumerable ways in which technology can be used to support differentiation. In this section, we focus on software programs, equipment, Web 2.0 tools, and assistive technology.

- *Software programs*: Currently on the market are a whole host of assessment-based, self-paced software programs that level students based on assessed prior knowledge, provide "appropriate" content for each student, and move through successive levels of difficulty and sophistication. One such program that we use in Oakwood, primarily for gifted math students, is ALEKS. ALEKS uses artificial intelligence to determine students' prior knowledge and readiness

and adapts content and pacing to instruct students on the content they are most equipped to learn.
- *Equipment*: Various technologies, such as document cameras, SMART Boards, and student response systems can be used to help provide differentiation within the classroom. For example, document cameras (tools to project images of two- and three-dimensional opaque objects on a screen) can project student writing samples for mini-lessons on revising for vivid verbs. Virtual manipulatives available in the SMART Board (interactive whiteboard) gallery can enhance math instruction for tactile or kinesthetic learners. Student response systems (remote clickers that allow students to respond individually to prompts or questions so their input is immediately visible on a screen) allow teachers to gauge students' understanding during a lesson and adjust instruction accordingly. Having such equipment, however, does not in itself guarantee differentiation. Some teachers use technology to teach all students the same content the same way. It is imperative that technology be used to provide students with multiple ways to learn content that is appropriate for them. Each general education classroom in Oakwood is outfitted with both a document camera and a SMART Board to support instruction. This major technological initiative in our district has been a main focus of permanent improvement funding. In addition to providing the equipment, we have invested in providing numerous differentiated professional development opportunities for teachers using these new tools (see Chapter 4 for professional development).
- *Web 2.0 tools*: *Web 2.0* is a phrase used to refer to interactive web features and applications, such as social networking sites, blogs, wikis, media-sharing sites, cloud computing, and free shareware, such as Google Docs, that allows multiple users to author, contribute to, and revise content simultaneously. Like the equipment mentioned above, Web 2.0 tools do not necessarily promote differentiation, but they can be used creatively by teachers to provide differentiated learning opportunities for students. For example, a class can collaboratively develop a wiki (a website on which multiple authors can collaboratively create, change, and arrange Internet content) for a specific unit of study. The teacher can assign responsibility for various pieces of content to students or student groups based on their interest, or the teacher can tier the sophistication and complexity of the required content contribution based on students' readiness. At the end of the wiki development project, the class has a collaboratively authored

website that can be used for review of the content and as a resource for future classes that study the content.
- *Assistive technology*: Assistive technology refers to any device used to aid students with special needs—for example, speech recognition software, sip-and-puff input devices, graphics tablets, text-to-speech devices, and Braille writers. The number and types of assistive tools available are ever-increasing, so a thorough examination of this topic is beyond the scope of this chapter. Technology can be invaluable for providing equitable access to core curricula for students with disabilities.

For more information about using technology in the differentiated classroom, see:

- Amy Benjamin. (2005). *Differentiated instruction using technology: A guide for middle & high school teachers*. Larchmont, NY: Eye On Education.

Differentiated Programming

While all students require differentiated content, instructional practices, and assessment practices to maximize their learning, some groups of students, such as students with disabilities, English language learners (ELLs), and gifted students, may require more significant accommodations and modifications. This may seem incredibly obvious; in fact, it is so obvious that it is often taken for granted. There are myriad models for providing specialized services for these groups. Our purpose here is not to evaluate the various models or to recommend specific ones. Rather, we want to emphasize that these programs should be seen not as separate entities isolated from the general education program, but rather as parts of the larger systemic approach to differentiating learning to meet *all* students' needs. Schools and districts need to think in terms of *differentiated universal education*. This term may seem like an oxymoron, but we use it to emphasize that *all* students (universally) should have access to quality, core instruction that is differentiated to meet their needs. This conceptual shift underscores the idea that different students require different approaches and services to maximize their potential—regardless of whether they are "regular ed" or "special ed" or "gifted" or "ELL." This is what we mean by differentiated universal education.

Summary

The purpose of this chapter is to emphasize that differentiation is much bigger than a series of strategies that individual teachers do inside of their closed classrooms. Differentiation, rather, must be viewed systemically across a school's or district's programming, and building and district leaders are key to making this happen. Differentiation is a commitment to utilizing assessment, instructional approaches and materials (including technology), and programming to meet the needs of all students. The focus must be much broader than an individual teacher's classroom. These are decisions and investments made at the building and district level that affect what happens in *all* classrooms.

References

Colburn, A. (2000). An inquiry primer. *Science Scope*, Special Issue (March), 42–44.
Popham, W. J. (2008). *Transformative assessment*. Alexandria, VA: ASCD.
Tomlinson, C. A. (2010a). The demographics, research, and ethics of differentiated instruction. ASCD Annual Conference, San Antonio, TX, March 6.
Tomlinson, C.A. (2010b). Personal communication, June 11.

7

Communicate! Communicate! And Then Communicate Some More!

> ### *This chapter will*
>
> 1. identify various stakeholder groups that need to be informed about differentiation
> 2. identify what each stakeholder group needs to know about differentiation
> 3. identify various methods of communication and provide examples of them

Three secrets

There are three secrets to success in building a culture of differentiation in your school and district:

1. Communication
2. Communication
3. Communication

> Speech is power: speech is to persuade, to convert, to compel. It is to bring another out of his bad sense into your good sense.
> —Ralph Waldo Emerson

As with any change you might be introducing and promoting in your organization, as school leaders you need to convince your listeners why that change is necessary. Articulating a sense of urgency is an imperative, ongoing step in successfully implementing change.

When communicating our plan to enculturate differentiation in our school and district, we ask ourselves the following questions:

- Which stakeholders need to be informed?
- What do they need to know?
- What methods will be used to inform them?

Which stakeholders need to be informed?

The first step we take is to determine which groups we want to communicate with. Communicating openly with these groups will open the door for earlier understanding, buy-in, ownership, and support of the concept. We identified the following stakeholder groups who need to be kept informed about our differentiation plans.

Teachers

Certainly establishing a positive culture of differentiation throughout the building and district will directly impact the teachers because we will be asking them to think about their work differently. The teachers are the ones in the trenches, working with the students every day. We will be holding them accountable for putting these concepts into place. We will be giving the teachers the tools for their tool bag—of course, not all the tools, but at least a hammer and a few nails, and the addresses of a few hardware stores where they can continually fill the rest of their tool bag.

Students

Surprisingly, this is a group of stakeholders that can be easily overlooked when communicating about differentiation. Although the information that is shared with students will vary from the secondary level to the elementary level, students need to be informed about the basics of differentiation and how they will benefit.

Parents

Keeping parents abreast of any hot topic must always be a top priority. Parents will certainly want to be informed about anything that we may be planning or implementing that will impact their children. As leaders, we must be ready and willing to help the parents build an understanding of the concept of differentiation—district-wide and school-wide, as well as inside the classroom. Although we may not be able to communicate with all the parents, the ones we do address will share the news with their friends and neighbors. It is our job to be certain that the news they share is accurate and positive.

Administrators

One or two administrators in a district (no matter how small or large) cannot effectively accomplish differentiation on their own. Sharing of the old and new successes and failures is a key part of the process. We are all in the same boat—it is essential that we are all paddling in the same direction, with the same type of oar.

Board of Education

This is another stakeholder group that may be inadvertently overlooked. However, this group is the liaison to the community. This is a group that we *must* include and keep in the loop regarding the process and progress of the implementation of differentiation.

What do they need to know?

Just as our teachers differentiate their instruction to specific groups of students, building and district leaders must differentiate their communication to specific groups of stakeholders. Each of the identified groups needs information about the concept of differentiation; some groups need more details than others, and some groups need different vocabulary than others.

Teachers

As building and district leaders, we need to communicate with teachers quite a bit about differentiation. We must explain what differentiation is all about and clearly *show* them what it looks like in terms of the process, content, and product. This needs to be defined, examples need to be shared, and opportunities for practice need to be provided and encouraged.

As we communicate our direction and expectations regarding differentiation, we must treat each other as professionals. Here we can and should use *educationese* in a professional manner. It is the building and district leaders' responsibility that our teachers understand what differentiation is and why we are so involved in it. Teachers must clearly comprehend that we are here to support them as they try new techniques and strategies: *It is okay to try and fail. We will still support you as you fail, and we will help you get back on your feet to try again.*

Similar to what we explain to parents and students, teachers must understand that we do not expect them to differentiate for their students 100% of the time. (They are relieved to know this is not our expectation.)

Students

As explained earlier, the level of information that is shared with students will depend on their level of schooling and maturity. Students do not necessarily need to be taught about the concept of differentiation, but they should know that a variety of help and assistance is available to them. If given too much information, some students may opt to use the concept as an easy way out of a challenging assignment, while others may take the opposite approach by taking on a difficult challenge for which they may not be ready. What students can expect is to be treated fairly, and fair treatment may vary from individual to individual.

Secondary students need to understand that we consider it our responsibility to prepare them for their next level of education. Because we do not know what experiences they will have in college, we will use a variety of instructional techniques, including relatively traditional instruction. Like their parents, students need to understand that alternatives will not be provided all the time.

Parents

Communication with parents needs to be clear, informative, and not overly complicated. Consider your reaction if someone were to explain to you the technical details of flying a rocket ship to Mars. You probably would be confused and overwhelmed if you were told how the current space-propulsion technologies were affected by the use of hot plasma, which were heated by radio waves and controlled by a magnetic field. However, you would want to know some general details about the mission, such as where the rocket ship would be traveling, why the mission was being undertaken, what steps the astronauts would take to get there, and how long the trip was expected to last. Perhaps you might even be curious about the backgrounds of the astronauts traveling on the mission.

When communicating with parents, we must remember that they are not educators. We cannot speak in *educationese*, at the risk of overwhelming them. The more overwhelmed and confused the parents are, the less chance that they will understand and support our mission.

When talking about differentiation or any new change to parents, it is helpful to begin with the big picture and explain *why* we are choosing to move in this direction. As parents become more comfortable with the topic over time, more specific details can be explained. Whether or not the school or district tracks students based on their ability, parents can expect their children to be exposed to a variety of teaching strategies, choices on reading passages, options for assignments, and so on. They can expect that teachers will provide learning experiences for their children to meet them where they are and take them forward from there. It is very important that the parents understand that differentiation does not happen 24/7. There is often still a need for whole-class instruction and activities.

Parents need to understand that differentiation is an evolving, systematic process. Administrators and teachers are continually collaborating to find new ideas to meet the needs of their students. The process may not be perfect today, but it will be better tomorrow and even better the next day.

Administrators

The leaders of the district and buildings must have a common understanding of differentiation. As leaders, we must also recognize that we do not always have the answers—but we need to know where to find those answers. Constant communication with each other on our findings of best practices, new publications, and professional development opportunities must be a priority. As mentioned earlier, no one administrator can successfully enculturate differentiation throughout the district alone; district and building administrators must work together to steer the ship in the same direction.

Board of Education

Every school district's Board of Education varies. Therefore, each district leader will need to determine the level of information that the board members should have. At a minimum, they should be as aware of the direction that the district is moving in as the parents. In our district, we have chosen to give the Board of Education a more in-depth awareness, perhaps not as deep as the teachers', but deeper than the parents'.

What methods will be used to inform them?

The content to be shared with each stakeholder group has been differentiated, so it only makes sense to differentiate the process by which the information is shared. In this portion, a variety of types, forms, and vehicles for communicating with the stakeholder groups will be explained. When appropriate, examples will be provided.

Teachers

As mentioned above, communication with teachers must be frequent and ongoing. As district and building administrators, we must be consistent and persistent with our message and expectations. Since, obviously, we know where the teachers work, it is fairly easy to deliver the ongoing message.

Establishing differentiation as a standing agenda item at our monthly faculty meetings can force us to dive deeper each month. Meaningful faculty meetings provide excellent opportunities to have rich, valuable conversations regarding progress, concerns, and best practices of differentiation. We often start our faculty meetings by sharing recent articles or video clips by experts, and our own teachers have often presented their experiences as conversation starters; their peers need to hear it from teachers rather than the administration. Teachers—perhaps the building's gifted or intervention specialist or a teacher who took a risk in the classroom—may present their success *or failure* in describing the risk they took.

Weekly or daily electronic newsletters sent to the teaching staff can easily include subtle, or not so subtle, topics relating to differentiation. Included in these staff weeklies or dailies can be praise of individual teachers for their successes in differentiating instruction. The more walk-throughs we conduct in our buildings, the more easily we have been able to praise our teachers in this manner. It is contagious—everyone wants to be praised. (See Figure 7.1 for an excerpt from an electronic weekly update sent to all staff at our junior high school.)

As another way of recognizing teachers' efforts in their classrooms, we have learned to never underestimate the value of a good old-fashioned handwritten note left in a teacher's mailbox. These are short, simple, and often greatly appreciated by the recipient. (Figure 7.2 is a sample note left in one teacher's mailbox.)

As mentioned in Chapter 4, talking with individual teachers at the beginning of the school year to set goals and at the end of the school year to review goals provides excellent opportunities to gauge the staff's comfort level in differentiating instruction. These conversations open the door for deeper and richer discussions with our teachers about their next steps with differentiation. In all such conversations, we must be certain we know our individual staff members. For the best results, we communicate with each type of teacher differently. As leaders, we choose the best style for that individual teacher.

In our district, we focus a great deal of time and energy on new teachers entering the district. Our district holds a week-long orientation for new teachers in early August of each year. Because questions about differentiation are part of our interview process for new teachers, they come to us with at least a basic understanding of differentiation and some experience utilizing differentiation strategies in the classroom. Part of orientation is acclimating new faculty and staff to our district goals, including the district's major, long-term focus on differentiation. All new teachers are given a copy of Carol Ann Tomlinson's book *The Differentiated Classroom: Responding to the Needs of All Learners*. During orientation, we also introduce newcomers to the expectation that all teachers write a professional goal related to differentiation each year (see Chapter 5). We encourage new teachers to work with their assigned mentors, with whom they begin meeting during orientation week, on using the self-assessment rubric and choice board to create their differentiation goal (which includes their choice of professional development on differentiation).

Whichever the method of communication, teachers need to be exposed to differentiation constantly. Training and professional development opportunities are made available at the school, or teachers are encouraged to access them elsewhere. Teachers are also encouraged to collaborate with each other, join professional learning communities, and visit other schools within or outside the district. All the answers will certainly not be provided through a few faculty meetings and weekly newsletters. As building and district leaders, we must remember that this stakeholder group is the most important one when it comes to following through on the expectation of delivering differentiated instruction.

Students

We communicate the concept of differentiation to our students in a basic manner. We may offer information to our students at such group programs as student orientations and beginning-of-the-year assemblies. We also encourage

FIGURE 7.1 Staff Newsletter

Jacks Facts

Oakwood Junior High School
January 10, 2008

Mark Your Calendar...

1/11	Success Breakfast Nomination Forms Due to Dawne		3:30 pm
1/14	Leadership Team Meeting	Office	11:50 am
1/14	Technology Meeting	Smith	3:30 pm
1/14	Board of Ed Meeting	BOE	7:30 pm
1/15	OJH/Rotary Student of Month forms due to DW by 9:00 am		
1/15	**Brief mandatory staff meeting**	**Library**	**Beg of Lunch**
1/16, 17, 18	Exams		
1/17	Student Recognition Meeting	135	10:00 am
1/17	OJH English Meeting	TBA	1:15 pm
1/18	Last day of 3rd 6 Weeks		
1/19	OJH Wrestling Duals	OJH	8:00 am
1/21	Martin Luther King Jr. Day—No School		
1/22	Grades Due by 6:00 pm		
1/23	**Success Breakfast**	**Café**	**7:00 am**
1/23	IAT	Fickert	11:45 am
1/23	Social Studies Dept Materials Review		3:45 pm
1/30	OJH Staff Meeting	Library	11:45 am
2/1	OJH/Rotary Student of Month	DCC	7:00 am

Did You Know???

- Amanda Ammer spearheaded the Lumberjack Leaders fundraiser, which raised over $1200 for the Make A Wish Foundation? Great job!
- Leslie Blythe has been giving up her lunchtime and after school hours to help her students finish their gym bags? Thanks, Leslie!
- Ann Whitehair and Amanda Ammer very successfully organized this year's Spelling Bee?
- We have frogs at OJH?!!
- Debbie Smith has been organizing Film Club in Kim Gilbert's room during lunch? Check the calendar and listen to the announcements of the movie times.
- Kristin Bull has been doing some great things to help our Oakwood students? She works with kids before school, after school, during lunch, and any other time available. Have you met Kristin yet—it's well worth your time!
- John Loomis and Tom Griffith open their doors every day during lunch to provide our students with a safe and enjoyable environment for kids to eat? Thanks, John and Tom.
- We have Rocket Scientists in Industrial Arts class?!!

FIGURE 7.1 Staff Newsletter *(continued)*

Brief Staff Meeting—Tuesday, 1/15/08—Library

Joe and I will hold a very brief staff meeting with all OJH and OHS staff members. This will be a mandatory meeting where we will share the newly adopted Bullying Policy. We will begin at 11:50 am. Thanks for flexing your schedule on this day.

Brief Staff Meeting—Tuesday, 1/15/08—Library

Success Breakfast—1/23/08

Please remember to nominate those deserving students for the upcoming Success Breakfast on 1/23/08. Those nomination forms are due to Dawne by 3:30 tomorrow (Friday). Thank you!

Oakwood Duals Wrestling Meet

Mark your calendars for next Saturday (1/19) for a rare home wrestling meet. At 8:00 am our wrestlers will take the mat in their home meet. Hopefully you can make it sometime that morning to support our wrestlers.

Web Pages

Reminder—keep those web pages up-to-date with pages that are easy to navigate!

New Copiers!

We hope you are enjoying the new copiers! So far I have heard very positive reviews.

Exam Week—1/16, 1/17, 1/18

Be certain to closely review the schedule you recently received. If you have any questions, please let me know.

Parent Contacts

In addition to all the many positive and not-so-positive contacts you make with parents throughout the year, please be certain that contact is made with parents of any student who is in danger of receiving a D or F for a specific grading period. Please make this contact early enough for that student to bring his/her grade up before the end of the grading period.

Communication to Parents—Groups/Clubs/Etc.

Upcoming Newsletters and LINX are outstanding ways to notify parents of upcoming events and important information regarding your groups and clubs. If there is any information that you would like to include in the weekly OJH LINX, please submit that to Dawne.

FIGURE 7.2 Note to Teacher

A note from Dan Weckstein . . .

Paul,
I enjoyed sitting in your class this morning. I really like the way that you shared the different ways of solving the same problem. (The kids also seemed to value this—shown by their requests for you to do more of the same.)

Great job differentiating your instruction and explanations.

Keep it up!
Dan

Oakwood City School District
Academic excellence since 1908

---

our teachers to talk with their students in their classrooms about differentiation throughout the year. The expectation is that our teachers are the main conduit of information to students regarding differentiation in the classroom. Students are not given a written guarantee of how they will be taught every day, but they will gain confidence that they will be taught by a variety of methods and they will be able to show their mastery in a variety of ways.

Inside Oakwood

Third-grade teacher Susan Lange is very candid with her students about the differentiation they can expect in her classroom. Here Susan explains how she frames differentiation for her students:

We talk in the beginning of the year, when we're building classroom community, about how everyone's different. We talk about all the ways we're different, and we celebrate and value our differences.

I explain to students that it's my job as their teacher to help each person be the best person they can be. We do a multiple intelligences assessment, so each student knows her/his strengths. I use this when I plan lessons—trying to present content in a variety of ways to match students' best ways to learn.

We also do a learning styles inventory. I use it to group students. For example, if they are tactile/kinesthetic, I might have them do some acting to develop their [reading] fluency or even to learn a spelling skill. The visual learners are put together to use bright colors to make a poster of information to be learned. The auditory learners may be asked to write a rap or song lyrics with the information. I also use tiered homework assignments, sometimes based on learning styles (or sometimes difficulty or content).

I try to assess students in the way they learned the material. When I give them different assessments, I remind them that I test them differently because they learn differently.

Besides teaching to the multiple intelligences, I also explain to them that we all have different abilities in different areas of life. Some people are great soccer players. Those who aren't but want to be know that they need some additional practice on their soccer skills. I'm like the soccer coach who provides the extra practice. Sometimes the extra practice is a helping thing, or time after school, or working with another teacher. These different levels of ability are to be valued—or else we'd all be the same. We try to celebrate one another's achievements, abilities, and differences.

Because of Susan's approach, her students and their parents know that not all students will be doing the same work the same way and taking the same assessments. Parents are supportive, and students feel valued because they know that Susan respects student differences and does her best to support all her learners.

◆ ◆ ◆ ◆ ◆ ◆ ◆ ◆ ◆

Parents

Whether at an assembly, at a small parent meeting, in writing, or in an informal conversation, we must remember to communicate with our students' parents in layman's terms. They are not educational experts, and they must be made to feel as comfortable as possible with the information they are receiving.

Opportunities to have these discussions and presentations are usually built into our calendar. The concept of differentiation can be a constant agenda item at all Parent Teacher Organization meetings, Parent Advisory Council meetings, conferences, open houses, and coffees/teas. Every occasion that we have an audience focused on us is an opportunity to reiterate our message and vision of differentiation.

Quarterly, monthly, or weekly newsletters (electronic or hard copy), newspaper articles, and website entries provide additional valuable avenues for communicating information and progress on differentiation in our schools and district. We use these venues to provide general information, summarize common questions that have come up at the abovementioned meetings, and promote the progress that our schools have made. (Figure 7.3 shows an excerpt from a sample newsletter from one of our elementary schools.)

We, as district and building leaders, should not be the only ones to communicate with the parents. Teachers and gifted and intervention specialists are excellent candidates to speak about their individual classes or on behalf of the staff. Furthermore, teachers can write interesting, informative, meaningful articles for parents to read in the newsletters. In these articles, teachers can communicate their differentiation styles, strategies, and opportunities to parents. (Figure 7.4 shows an excerpt from an eighth-grade English teacher's weekly newsletter to her students' parents.)

Administrators

Regular administrators' meetings, with identified time to discuss progress on differentiation, have proven to be extremely valuable opportunities for our district and building leaders. Equally valuable has been an administrators' professional learning community developed exclusively to enculturate differentiation throughout our district. As described in Chapter 3, this nonnegotiable timeframe has provided for priceless discussions, sharing of successes and failures, and opportunities to conduct walk-throughs in all the school buildings.

Board of Education

At each Board of Education meeting in our school district, board members and the community are treated to a curriculum showcase. These showcases highlight great things happening in the school buildings or district-wide. These provide for yet another opportunity for our performing teachers to share samples of the creative, differentiated lessons going on in their classrooms. While directly informing our community and Board of Education, these presentations empower our teachers while they celebrate their successes. Listed on pages 115 and 116 are the curriculum showcases for the 2007–2008 school year:

FIGURE 7.3 Excerpt from Newsletter to Parents

Differentiation: What? Why? How? (Amanda Ammer)

Our district's recently adopted mission statement asserts, "Doing what is best for students is our guiding principle." In order to attain this principle, the statement continues, our community will utilize "the resources, support, expertise, and experiences needed for all students to achieve." Indeed, the young people in this community come to school with unique and diverse talents and needs, and our teachers work alongside them as they meet with success.

This process does not happen automatically, nor does it happen by chance. Our teachers work daily to accommodate academic diversity in the planning, practice, and assessment phases of instruction. This conscientious approach to learning is called differentiation. Differentiation is an ongoing process that teachers use to help each child achieve using his or her abilities to their fullest potential. Furthermore, differentiation is named as a linchpin in our district's gifted services. You have likely heard your child's teachers, and perhaps your child, use this phrase. But what does it really mean?

What is differentiation? In education, differentiation is defined as "modifying content, process, and/or product according to student interest, readiness, and learning profile" (Tomlinson, 1999). In other words, teachers purposefully examine and consider the students' prior experiences, current achievement and ability levels, as well as how students learn best. This information is then used when planning what to teach, how to teach it, and how to measure what students have learned.

There are two points to note in considering differentiation: First, as a minimum requirement, all students are required to meet state standards. These standards are not negotiable. Second, differentiation is not individualized instruction for each student every day. It takes place over time and throughout many topics.

Why should teachers use differentiation? Simply put, what students bring to school as learners impacts how they learn (Tomlinson, 2003). Our district's core value of respect echoes this rationale for teachers implementing differentiation: "It is important that we seek ways to demonstrate our understanding of and appreciation for differences among us." In addition, educational research reinforces the elements of differentiation. For example, brain research confirms that new learning must be connected to earlier learning (Jensen, 1998). Also, the transfer of knowledge to long-term memory requires active processing of information (Jensen, 1998), which differentiation encourages.

How does differentiation look? Differentiation in the classroom can range from subtle to more open techniques. Students are often not aware of how a teacher observes interests, readiness levels, and learning profiles. One of the best ways to find out about differentiation in the classroom is to ask your child's teacher. He or she can easily explain the role differentiation plays in the classroom.

FIGURE 7.4 Eighth-Grade English Newsletter

Gilbert's Gab
Week of 9/22/08

8th English–regular

WOW! What a crazy week we have all experienced! I hope you have power. I am still living in the world of darkness in the evening! I have a whole new respect for our early ancestors.

This week we continued our study of nonfiction and discussed the Mexican/American experience in "Barrio Boy." The selection illustrated an overall theme of overcoming adversity and how that helps to build character. Next week we will start our study of Dr. Martin Luther King, Jr. and create peace trading cards for the Dayton Literary Award Celebration to take place in a couple of weeks! Our cards will express notions of peace to be spread throughout the world.

Did you know students have a variety of opportunities to learn and master a skill or lesson? **Differentiation** or modification will be used throughout the year in such cases as pretests in grammar, RRL choices throughout the year, student-driven projects, and as always—extra credit opportunities.
*More information to follow!

SPEECH & DRAMA

This week, we completed most of the travel speeches. I am thoroughly impressed with the delivery, poise, and enthusiasm along with each demonstration I have seen in every speech. The places and vacation stories are simply amazing! Next week, we will start oral interpretation of children's literature. Students will have the opportunity to read their favorite children's book using voice, projection, inflection, pitch, and rate.

Composition

This week we started brainstorming for our next major composition, a survivor essay. Students have the job of writing a process paper to include details on how to survive on a deserted island. The award-winning film CASTAWAY has several ideas to help get the creative juices flowing. The final draft will be due in a week and a half.

*A weekly syllabus is posted on my web page!
- Email me for any questions or concerns: gilbert.kim@oakwood.k12.oh.us
- Check out my new web page! http://www2.oakwood.k12.oh.us/~gilbert_kim
- 9/23 OJHS Pep Rally 2:45
- 9/24 Early Release 11:43
- 10/1 Homecoming Parade and bonfire
- 10/3 End of first marking period
- 10/6 PTO Open House Cookout 6:00
- 10/6 Open House 7:00

Oakwood Board of Education Curriculum Showcases

September 2007:
Oakwood Junior High language arts teacher Susanne King will share with the board her use of differentiation strategies in the classroom, including tiered assessments. She will be leading a professional development session this year for Oakwood teachers on tiered assessments.

October 2007:
Kelly Colson, high school math teacher and Jensen brain-based learning specialist, will share with the board her leadership of the "Facilitating Learning" professional learning community (PLC). PLCs are groups of educators who meet regularly to study a topic, implement new strategies, and reflect on their effectiveness. The audience for this group includes educators who will serve as facilitators for the PLCs that Oakwood Schools is offering this school year. These PLCs will focus on various aspects of differentiation—one of our district's goals—as it relates to responding to our student's readiness, interests, and strengths in the classroom.

November 2007:
Differentiation is about reaching all students' needs. Students with disabilities learn best when intervention specialists and general classroom teachers work together to provide instruction at the student's readiness level. Teachers Bryan Ellis, Rachel Keyes, Sarah Martin, Ann Whitehair, and Linda Hallinan will present to the board their work on collaboration and co-teaching between intervention specialists and general classroom teachers.

December 2007:
Peggy Holton, Oakwood High School prevention/intervention counselor, will present information regarding the executive summary of the South Suburban Teen Alcohol and Other Drug Prevention report.

January 2008:
Smith School second-grade teacher Sandy Zipes and students will showcase our Weatherbug tool that was installed this fall and funded by the Oakwood Schools Education Foundation. Our Weatherbug station is located on the roof of Smith School and provides live video feed of weather and a host of meteorological data, including temperature, atmospheric pressure, precipitation, wind direction, wind speed, humidity, and dew point. Weatherbug can

be used in grades K–12 and by all Oakwood community members. Go to http://weather.weatherbug.com/ and put in your zip code! The Weatherbug service also provides links to Weatherbug data from other schools around the world, as well as lesson plans and video conferences with meteorologists and climatologists.

February 2008:
Smith Elementary art teacher Christina Gluck will share with the board ways in which she integrates the academic content standards into art instruction and how she differentiates art instruction to meet students' readiness levels, interests, and strengths. She will share with the board samples of students' work.

March 2008:
Designing instruction to meet students' learning profiles (learning modalities and multiple intelligences) is an important form of differentiation. Smith Elementary sixth-grade teacher Mary Kay Buffington will share with the board her class's project about daily life in ancient Egypt. Students learned what life was like for five social classes in ancient Egypt, and they worked in groups to create interactive dramatizations (using props, costumes, and audience involvement) to represent what they learned. The presentation will show how the project addressed students' multiple intelligences, and the teacher will share with the board a student skit, the project rubric, photos from the project, and her final assessment of student learning.

♦ ♦ ♦ ♦ ♦ ♦ ♦ ♦ ♦

"Ugh, another curriculum showcase about differentiation?!" This is our favorite remark made by a local newspaper reporter who attends all Board of Education meetings. Given our intention of keeping the Board of Education and community informed of our progress with differentiation, we seem to be succeeding based on this reporter's remark!

Other ways to keep the Board of Education abreast of the happenings in the buildings are limitless. For example, we invite a board representative to attend Parent Teacher Organization meetings, include the Board of Education in all parent and staff newsletter mailings, both electronic and hard copy, and invite board members to participate in faculty meeting discussions.

Summary

Enculturating differentiation in our buildings and district is a long and sometimes painful process. But with thorough, well-planned communication to our identified stakeholder groups, the process becomes much less painful and perhaps even enjoyable.

8

Staffing

This chapter will

1. illustrate the importance of hiring the best staff for your building
2. provide sample interview questions for hiring teachers who are knowledgeable about and committed to differentiation and doing what is best for their students
3. share ideal responses to look for during interviews
4. demonstrate the importance of orientation and mentoring new teachers

---

I have come to the frightening conclusion that I am
the decisive element in the classroom.
It is my personal approach that creates the climate.
It is my daily mood that makes the weather.
As a teacher, I possess tremendous power
to make a child's life miserable or joyous.
I can be a tool of torture or an instrument of inspiration.
I can humiliate or humor, hurt or heal.
In all situations it is my response that decides
whether or not a crisis will be escalated or de-escalated,
and a child humanized or dehumanized.
I am part of a team of educators
creating a safe, caring and positive learning environment for students
and teaching them in a manner that ensures success
because all individuals are capable of learning.

—Dr. Haim G. Ginott

Hiring teachers and support staff—this is the most important duty that we have as building and district leaders. The people we hire are going to work with their students behind the classroom door each period, every day, year after year. The principal, the department chair, or the mentor certainly cannot accompany these new teachers all the time. Therefore, it is absolutely critical that administrators see that their buildings are staffed with *the best*—not the second-best, or the pretty good for now, but *the best* staff available.

Sometimes very few applicants are available for the posted position. It could be that no applicant can measure up. If this is the case, a decision must be made to start the search process over if time permits, hire a long-term substitute for the year, or fill the position with the best available applicant with the most potential. If the third option is chosen, this would be the time to take the chance on a gut feeling, perhaps with a recent graduate who may not have shone in the interview, but has the drive and child-centered qualities to succeed in the classroom.

Often hiring does not get the emphasis it should. Sometimes the emphasis might be on getting the job finished, speeding up the process to get to the next thing on the ever-growing list. Ultimately, this method will cheat our students. It is simply not fair to our students to neglect putting the appropriate amount of time and effort into doing the most important task that we are assigned to do.

How Do You Hire *the Best*?

Hiring *the best* teachers is certainly not an easy task. It involves a number of steps and a select group of colleagues who are committed to the task. Broken down into the most simple plan, here is a five-step process to get the job done most effectively:

Step 1: Sifting through applications and résumés.

Whether it is completed by the building principal or the director of personnel, reviewing the multitude of applications that have been submitted for a specific job can be a daunting task. To make this task more manageable, prior to sifting through the applications is the time to clearly identify the needs of the building or department. Does the fourth grade need someone with a specific content expertise to complement its team of teachers? Does the high school science department need an expert in technology? After the specific needs have been identified, résumés and applications can be weeded out or pushed to the top. *Warning:* Be careful not to weed out too quickly—sometimes a high-quality applicant can be overlooked. Keep an open mind throughout the review.

Tip: A very useful technique is to make a three-minute telephone call to a neighboring school or district. Has it recently interviewed applicants for a similar position? Its second-place finalist may be the perfect fit for your building. This specific applicant's résumé may not be in your stack of applications, but you may well end up recruiting and attracting that person to your district.

A résumé or application can give a lot of information, and a cover letter gives the reader a small taste of the applicant's writing skills and use of language, but they cannot provide details regarding personality and attitude. *Warning:* Sometimes applicants even have "help" filling out applications. Hence, the necessity of an interview with a hand-selected team of staff members.

Step 2: Putting an interview team together.

In *From Good to Great,* Jim Collins (2001) refers to having the "right people on the bus." Finding and hiring those "right people" can become a less daunting task if you get a few qualified colleagues to ensure that the bus is going to be driven in the right direction. Those qualified colleagues are chosen because of where they are sitting on the bus and why and how they got to be in those seats.

In general terms, the interview team must be thoroughly knowledgeable about the current needs of the building or department. Teachers on an interview team may have a tendency to look for people like themselves. However, it is imperative that they know what the school or district is looking for. They need to know where the staff is weak and where it is strong. They must have the professionalism and courage to speak up for the applicant who will contribute to the school environment, not just the one they would prefer to work with. Like the ideal applicant, the members of the interview team must themselves be instructionally competent, child-centered, knowledgeable, personable, and committed to the belief that teachers hold the responsibility to help their students experience success.

In more specific terms for the building of an interview team, the following professionals should be at the table: the department chair, a department member, a special educator, and a building administrator. Depending on the level of the open position, additional stakeholder groups could be represented.

For example, if there is an opening for assistant principal, a parent, student, administrative assistant, and/or counselor may be selected to join the team. Moreover, more than one team may interview the same applicants at separate times.

Setting the expectations and ground rules for the interview team prior to the interviews is strongly advised. Even though these individuals were hand-selected because of their proven track record and priorities to do what is best for kids, reviewing the building's needs, strengths, and weaknesses is advised. Additionally, it is also advised to clearly explain to the team why they have been chosen to participate and that though their input will be highly valued, the final decision will lie in the hands of the administrators.

Step 3: Asking interview questions to gain insight into the candidates.

The key to hiring is to find the teacher who is all about students and students' learning, who has the special qualities and attitude and perspective to do whatever it takes for kids in the classroom. Those details need to come out during the interview. But those details may not come through unless quality questions are asked.

Knowledge of content and pedagogy is certainly necessary, but not sufficient. A special education teacher, for example, can be taught to write an individualized education plan (IEP). However, it is most difficult, nearly impossible, to teach that same teacher to be approachable and personable with students and colleagues and to be an advocate for students. That teacher's personal qualities and approach to dealing with students, colleagues, and parents must be demonstrated during the interview. And those intangibles can be seen by asking the right questions.

Any questions that allow for an open-ended response can provide a window into what the applicant is really like. These interview questions must get to what is *in the heart* of the applicant. When looking through that window, you want to see that the candidate has a positive attitude and is personable, motivated, caring, and student-centered. These qualities *can* be evaluated by asking the right questions. More important, they can be evaluated by closely listening to the responses. Asked a variety of open-ended questions, applicants have a blank slate on which to respond. A wide variety of sample open-ended questions and ideal responses follow:

Describe a lesson that you taught that was meaningful and successful.
(You want to hear about a lesson that the kids enjoyed *and* that they learned from. Perhaps you will hear how the teacher differentiated in some way. You don't want to hear just

that the kids loved the lesson and no detail about how they were challenged or benefited from the lesson.)

Describe how you help students solve academic problems in your class.
(This prompt gets to the level at which the teacher differentiates student involvement and expectations. A quality answer would include a variety of methods—providing a lot of help, leading the students to the answer by asking questions without providing the answer, leaving students to figure out the problems on their own, etc.)

Talk to us about your experience in working with students with special needs.
(This question is highly recommended in any teacher interview. It can tell the interview team about the applicant's experience and willingness to make accommodations—which necessitates differentiation. You will also want to hear about the applicant's experience or desire to collaborate with the special educator on how to best meet the needs of students. This response will provide a wealth of insight into the heart of the applicant.)

How do you assess your students and what do you do with the information?
(You want to hear about a variety of assessment mechanisms. This variety will be grounded in differentiation—differentiated assignments, differentiated rubrics, differentiated expectations, traditional testing—a smorgasbord of assessments. You want to hear about preassessments and formative assessments (including many of the details referred to in Chapter 6.) Although the term *differentiation* may not actually be used by the applicants, they should describe it in their response. As for what they do with the information, the applicant should mention that it is used to guide future classroom activities and instruction. If all the students understood the lesson, they move on. If they did not get it, the teacher reteaches in a different way because whatever was done the first time did not work, at least to the level of rigor that was initially set.)

Describe your most effective teaching strategies.
(This question ties back to what the building and department need—what they are hoping to hire. This is also an excellent prompt to gain insight into the applicant's experience and interest in differentiation.)

Give us five adjectives that best describe you.
(Ahhh . . . the age-old question. Like the last question, this one can help determine if the applicant will fit your needs. Additionally, this response will help the team to determine what the applicant is truly about—the kids or the job.)

What are you going to be doing five (or ten) years from now?
(Some might say the best response is, "I will still be [doing the job I'm applying for]." However, consider the big picture in your building or district. The response does not

have to specify the position that the candidate is applying for, as long as it includes something about kids—helping them learn, helping them succeed. Motivation is extremely valuable. Having a motivated team player, even if it is only for a short while, is priceless. This applicant could become a counselor or administrator, a leader in your building or district after a few years in the classroom, and that position may be even more valuable if it is indeed the right fit.)

We have also found that situational or scenario-based questions can be quite helpful in gauging an applicant's problem-solving techniques and talents. **A student in your class refuses to do his homework; how would you handle that? Two or three students in your third-period class have grasped the content quickly; what do you do with them as you teach the rest of the class?**

All these questions provide the opportunity for applicants to thoroughly discuss their experience with differentiation. This is certainly something that we look for during an interview. However, we fully understand that each applicant's lingo and language may not be what we use in our district. Many college students have not been thoroughly exposed to the term *differentiation*, and we must remember that we are looking for meaning, not just terms to be used.

When interviewing candidates for a building principalship or district leadership position, the interview team should ask similar types of questions. Among the many different responses, the interview team will want to hear details about the applicant's experience and dedication to differentiation and doing whatever it takes to help students experience success. A few sample questions follow:

Why and how do want your teachers to assess their students? What do you expect them to do with that data?

We have an ongoing district goal of implementing differentiation in all classrooms. What is differentiation to you? Why and when would it be used? How would you support this goal?

A parent calls to complain that her daughter is not being adequately challenged in her fourth-grade classroom. How do you respond?

Step 4: Discussing each applicant and hiring *the best*!

Every building and department may have its own unique methods of sharing thoughts and opinions regarding individual candidates. One effective method to illustrate the strengths and weaknesses of each candidate is to create a list of pros and cons, as well as any questions for individual candidates. During this process, it can be difficult to articulate a gut feeling, yet it should not be ignored. That gut feeling, especially if it is a positive one, may be because of the candidate's motivation or personal relations with people. Asking the team member to articulate a gut feeling will help the rest of the team to understand that viewpoint.

Hiring *the best* is not a simple task. The winning candidate must be competent and rigorous, who will come to the classroom committed to doing what is best for students, convinced that all students can learn, and determined to make that happen by creating an environment that will maximize student learning and allow every student to experience success.

The topic of differentiation is but one piece of the puzzle during an interview. Certainly there are more issues to discuss during the interview process, but the applicants' knowledge and experience with differentiated instruction, their ability to articulate that knowledge during an interview, and their demonstrated openness to do what is best for kids will give deep insight into their motivation and talents. This insight will provide a glimpse into their heart, attitude, and personal qualities that will determine their *willingness* to differentiate, to do whatever it takes to meet the needs of their individual students.

Step 5: Orienting and mentoring the newly hired teachers.

Once the new teacher has been hired, the orientation and mentoring programs must take over.

New Teacher Orientation

Throwing a new teacher into a den of wolves is a concept of the past. Especially for a teacher fresh out of college, who has been exposed only to education courses and student teaching, a new job can be bewildering or even overwhelming. Orientation to the school and district is the kick-off of the new teacher's career or the fresh start to a veteran's career. The school's orientation program for new teachers provides the first impression—the golden opportunity to share priorities and expectations, to attract and retain the newest members of the team for the rest of their career.

New teachers (both new to the profession and new to the district) must be given the opportunity and assistance to become acclimated to their new work environment. Our district has a four-day orientation program jam-packed with activities, workshops, question and answer sessions, tutorials, and more. This four-day program could legitimately be even longer and more beneficial to the new teachers because there is so much new information to share.

Throughout the orientation program, we model our own differentiation strategies with the newest members of our team. For example, we differentiate for readiness by requiring new hires who have never taught before to attend the entire orientation program, while experienced teachers who are new to our school or district are only required to attend certain portions of the program. We differentiate for interest by having new teachers select a workshop of their choice to attend on the fourth day of the program, and we differentiate for process by using a variety of activities to orient new teachers to the culture of our district.

One emphasis of the orientation program is to acclimate the new teachers to the school district and community. Time is spent reviewing the district's core values (see Chapter 2), the beliefs and driving principles behind our daily work. A full understanding of these core values will give new teachers the background to effectively develop formal and informal goals for their first year.

Another emphasis is to provide the new teachers with a cultural orientation to the district. A guided driving tour of the community to view the schools in the district, a few notable landmarks, different neighborhoods, and the best coffee shops is a helpful start, especially to those unfamiliar with the area. And just as helpful are the tales told along the way! We also give new teachers a review of local newspapers featuring recent articles written about the schools, district, and community. Articles in the school newspapers sometimes give the best taste of the teachers' new environment. This is a time to discuss what is surprising about the community, what is unique, and what teachers can expect in their new life here.

Beyond the core values and the reports in the local newspapers, new teachers need to know what is really going on in the district and the individual buildings. Orientation is the time to share with the newest members of the team the hot issues and key initiatives we all face and how to best address those issues. Differentiation, for example, though a crucial focus during our orientation, is only one of the many necessary topics for teachers new to the district. If too much time is spent on a topic like differentiation, other topics might become lost in the mix. New teachers first need to get into their classroom and gain knowledge about their students and their curriculum. They will clearly discover the priority that differentiation holds as they attend our district-wide professional development sessions, building meetings, and regular meetings with their mentor.

A significant amount of time (but never enough) is spent discussing and displaying technology. The Technology Department is heavily involved in this portion of the orientation, showing off the standard gadgets in the classroom as well as what might be available to the ambitious teacher. It is important not to gloss over the basics in technology, such as how to take attendance and how to input grades. These everyday tools have the potential to stress out even the most confident professionals; they must be mastered right away so on the first day of school the teacher is ready to roll.

A portion of orientation time is also spent covering the nuts and bolts of everyday life as a teacher in the district: teacher contracts, benefits, expenses and purchase orders, professional development plans, teachers' union introductions, and so on. Two and a half days are spent in our district covering the topics and activities described above. One half of the third day is spent in the buildings where the new teachers will be working—meeting with the principal and with their mentor and exploring their new classroom when time permits. A luncheon for new teachers, their mentors, and administrators is also held on the third day, providing a casual environment for getting to know each other. The fourth day is reserved for the new teachers to attend training workshops in technology, curriculum, or another area of their choice. These workshops demonstrate our commitment to differentiation in action and emphasize the priority we give to professional development.

New teachers walk away from our orientation program with their heads full of information and their hands full of valuable materials. Among several additional items, we give teachers their curriculum guide, a useful binder organized with details from the orientation program, Charlotte Danielson's *Enhancing Professional Practice*, and Carol Ann Tomlinson's *The Differentiated Classroom*. The expectation is for these materials to be digested at a future time, to be discussed with mentors, and to be resources for future meetings.

Although four days of orientation is a healthy period of time, it remains a challenge to fit everything in. Teachers who have gone through the program have suggested spending more time with technology training, more time in the individual buildings, more time reviewing available classroom materials, more time practicing how to input attendance records and grades . . . all while keeping the rest of the program intact. The difficulty of providing new teachers with all the information they need to know is one of the many reasons we have established our mentoring program.

Mentoring the New Teacher

The hiring process is complete; the orientation program has come and gone; now it is the mentor's job to be certain the new teacher makes it through the first year. Selecting the most effective mentor for each individual is an important task.

A district-wide Mentor Committee was formed in our district to emphasize the importance of the mentoring program and to streamline the process. Each building has a representative who is in communication with the district leader and the building principal. They all work together to find the best mentor partnerships and to encourage potential mentors to go through the proper training. The building representative also serves as a link for the mentor who has any questions or concerns along the way.

Who is the right mentor? A good mentor models positive interactions with colleagues, students, and parents, does good things for kids, and can push the new teacher in a positive direction. A strong mentor has the personality to be supportive, yet corrective, and is mature enough to guide a new teacher, some more directly than others. A requirement is to have the mentor in the same department, grade level, or curriculum area as the new teacher, but that is certainly not the only thing to consider. Strong mentors have a strong teaching background, which makes them an excellent source of knowledge about both content and pedagogy. Good mentors give 110%, participating in committees and after-school activities, making the school culture part of their being. They know they can also learn from the mentee, that a good collegial relationship can work both ways. Mentors must have also received professional development about what constitutes an effective mentoring environment.

It is not a coincidence that the right mentor has many of the same characteristics of a high-quality applicant.

Who is not the right mentor? A bad mentor can have a lasting negative impact on a new, impressionable teacher. Just because teachers have met the qualifications to be a mentor does not make them a quality mentor. Educators who are not strong in their content area or not strong pedagogically should not be considered to mentor a new teacher. A teacher with a negative attitude should not be considered for such a position. Misery loves company, and a poor outlook can be contagious, especially for a teacher looking to fit into a new environment.

How important is it to select the right mentor for your new teacher? When a recent first-year teacher was asked how important it is to have the right mentor, she responded, "SO IMPORTANT. You have to mesh and be able to work as a team. You have to have someone that works well with you, gets you, and understands your personality." Yet when another first-year teacher was asked the same question, she responded, "Not completely important. . . . There are a good number of teachers I feel comfortable going to both in my department and outside my department, which is nice. I really do feel as though I have many mentors in addition to my assigned one."

As administrators (and perhaps with the assistance of the Mentor Committee representative from the building), we do our best to select the right mentor for every new teacher. Sometimes, however, we fail to hit the target. To prepare for that infrequent case, it is beneficial to encourage additional department members to make connections with the new teachers. As the new teacher stated above, she felt that she could go to additional members of the staff for guidance, as if she had more than one mentor.

What role does the mentor play? The initial benefit of our mentor program is that it gives new teachers a connection in the building and district from the very beginning of their tenure. The new teachers know they can go to the mentor for answers—even to the most basic questions. The mentor can provide guidance about curriculum, technology, resources, culture, tradition, best practices, and more. In a nutshell, the role of the mentor is to guide the mentee through the first year.

After the first year, new teachers typically have found additional informal mentors, in addition to their official one. These additional mentors provide guidance and, more importantly, friendship. Of course, the new teacher often continues the informal mentoring (and friendship) with the original mentor long after the teacher's first year.

Summary

Imagine a high school coach of a competitive baseball team having the choice between a group of players with decent skills and a great deal of heart and desire to do what is best for the team, and a group of players with outstanding skills and egos that go along with those skills, players whose attitude is *I don't have to practice. If we lose, it was someone else's fault.* That coach is going to choose the players with heart and desire. They can practice their skills, and because of their dedication and motivation to succeed they will steadily improve and become the best as a team.

Motivation cannot be taught. Attitude, dedication, and a commitment to do what is best for students cannot be taught. Personable relations with colleagues, parents, and students cannot be taught. These are qualities and traits of *the best* teachers.

Hiring *the best* applicants is not a simple task, but it will pay priceless dividends over the years. Getting the right people on the bus, based on the needs of the building or department, will benefit the students and the community.

Once *the best* applicants have been hired, they must be welcomed into the community and supported. They must become a part of the family in a casual, yet professional setting. Through the orientation and mentoring process, *the best* candidates will become *the best* teachers and leaders.

References

Collins, J. (2001). *From good to great: Why some companies make the leap and others don't.* New York: Harper Business.

Danielson, C. (2007). *Enhancing professional practice: A framework for teaching.* 2nd ed. Alexandria, VA: ASCD.

Tomlinson, C. A. (1999). *The differentiated classroom: Responding to the needs of all learners.* Alexandria, VA: ASCD.

9
Jungle to Greenhouse

> **This chapter will**
>
> 1. provide a useful analogy to illustrate the need for differentiation
> 2. identify nine key strategies to implement differentiation in your school

Bringing It All Together

The newest member of our administrative team, Paul Waller, principal of Oakwood High School, clarifies the complicated concept of differentiation in this enlightening analogy:

♦ ♦ ♦ ♦ ♦ ♦ ♦ ♦ ♦ ♦

Going from a Jungle to a Greenhouse

As a past science teacher, when I think about teaching I often think in terms of ecosystems.

A classroom is a beautiful place, full of students with the potential to grow and blossom. I often think of a classroom in terms of a jungle. A jungle is a beautiful place as well. The diversity of life is amazing and at a first glance it might seem as if everything is thriving.

However, when we take a closer look, we notice that some of the plants are not doing so well. They might be shaded out from the sun and their growth is stunted, waiting for something to happen to a larger plant or tree that would allow light to penetrate the canopy. Large plants with aggressive root systems choke out seedlings as they try to take hold. Vines desperately climb the large trees in search of light while at the same time stealing important nutrients from the host.

A classroom without differentiation is much like a jungle. A classroom is a beautiful place, but if we look closer we see that the students whose learning styles match the pedagogy of the teacher do well while others may struggle and begin to wilt.

Now imagine going into a greenhouse: you will see many of the same plants that are in a jungle as well as plants from other ecosystems. They are *all* thriving. They are placed in conditions that are conducive to their individual light, water, and humidity needs. Additionally, they are not all grouped together in one place. If they were, only the plants that have those specific needs would survive.

Although a jungle is a beautiful place, it is not what we want our classrooms to be. We need to move classrooms from a jungle to a greenhouse. If teachers are differentiating their instruction and assessments to meet our students' needs and interests, all learners will thrive.

The next time you walk into a greenhouse, notice the diverse life and think of your diverse classrooms.

♦ ♦ ♦ ♦ ♦ ♦ ♦ ♦ ♦

It is our role, as building and district leaders, to be certain that our schools are made up of many greenhouses, not jungles. This task will keep us very, very busy—greenhouses require a significant amount of maintenance. And certainly we cannot do it by ourselves; our teachers must be the greenhouse managers. We must provide them with the tools and resources to properly maintain their multiple ecosystems.

If we had to melt this book down into its most elemental themes, here is what they would be:

Recognize the Importance of Differentiation

As readers learned in Chapter 1, our district has a culture of high standards and even higher expectations. But that certainly does not mean that the concepts and strategies discussed in this book are geared only for districts that are similar to Oakwood. Differentiated instruction is for *all* schools and districts, no matter the similarities or differences, no matter the socioeconomic status, no matter the location, and no matter the size.

Set Goals

Perhaps U.S. Army major general Charles C. Noble (1916–2003) said it best: "You must have long-term goals to keep you from being frustrated by short-term failures." Goals, tied directly to the district's vision, mission, and core values, must be clear and concise. Having too many goals, or goals that are vague and ambiguous, could result in steps backward or steps in a variety of directions. On the other hand, for everyone to successfully, systematically move forward in the same direction, having a small number of goals, clearly communicated to all stakeholders, will be most beneficial to the organization.

Learn Together

Anthropologist Margaret Mead is quoted as saying, "Never doubt that a small group of thoughtful, committed citizens can change the world; indeed, it's the only thing that ever has." The concept of a district administrative team working and learning together in a PLC in each other's buildings may be new to the reader. This has been one of the most effective and invigorating pieces of our journey. Walk-throughs in another building, Critical Friends discussions resulting in priceless advice, artifact sharing, book studies, and in-depth, rich conversations about strategies and philosophies—these have been a priority and have proven highly valuable.

Develop Teacher Leaders

In *The Differentiated School*, Tomlinson and colleagues (2008) describe the importance of teacher leadership in supporting and sustaining change: "Although a vital role of the building principal in bringing about second-order change is focusing and sustaining attention on a vision for change, it is the teachers who will have to do the hard work of change." It is these teacher leaders—respected by their peers, instructionally skilled and talented, and early adopters of differentiation—who will play a major role in carrying out the plan to successfully enculturate differentiation throughout the building and district.

Model Differentiation

Furthermore, the members of the administration *must* model differentiation in how they lead, how they evaluate, and how they provide professional development. In other words, walk the walk; don't just talk the talk.

Expect and Push

The title of this book succinctly states, "Differentiation is an expectation." A time will come when building and district leaders have to *push* teachers to embed differentiation in their teaching strategies. This becomes nonnegotiable. Evaluating differentiation and differentiating evaluation must become a regular part of the evaluation process. Oakwood's CORE Team, a group composed of teacher leaders and administrators—described thoroughly in Chapters 4 and 5—developed the many strategies and nonnegotiables to push our entire staff toward differentiation. Of course, this continues to be an ongoing process—tweaking our rubric and choice board, providing the most effective professional development, and more.

Think Systemically

Differentiation is a part of almost every instructional conversation and decision that occurs in Oakwood. Building and district leaders must think systemically about this concept. When selecting assessments, instructional approaches, materials, and technology, meeting the needs of *all* the students must be discussed. As noted in Chapter 6, some instructional approaches lend themselves to differentiation or are differentiated in nature (e.g., reading and writing workshops).

Communicate!

"The single biggest problem in communication is the illusion that it has taken place." George Bernard Shaw's quote points to a common error in implementing a culture of differentiation or, indeed, any change in an organization. Clearly articulating the reason for change and the benefits of that change is a step in implementation that must not be ignored. All stakeholders, including teachers, students, parents, administrators, and the Board of Education, must be included in the communication plan. There can never be too much communication with these stakeholders.

Hire *the Best*

Lawrence Bossidy, a highly regarded executive at General Electric and CEO of Honeywell Corporation, said it best: "I am convinced that nothing we do is more important than hiring and developing people. At the end of the day you bet on people, not on strategies." As clearly emphasized in Chapter 8, it is critical that building and district administrators hire *the best* staff they can find and then give them the appropriate tools, training, guidance, and opportunities not only to succeed, but to soar.

A Final Thought

When talking with fellow educators in our district, in neighboring communities, or at leadership conferences, we have been approached with the same question: "When will you stop focusing on differentiation?"

To us, the answer is simple:
We will stop focusing on differentiation when it has become as natural as breathing and as automatic as taking attendance.

> Differentiation isn't a fad.
> Differentiation isn't a trend.
> *Differentiation isn't an invitation.*
>
> Differentiation is meeting the needs of our students.
> Differentiation is doing what is best for our students.
> *Differentiation is an expectation.*

Reference

Tomlinson, C. A., Brimijoin, K., and Narvaez, L. (2008). *The differentiated school: Making revolutionary changes in teaching and learning.* Alexandria, VA: ASCD.

For Product Safety Concerns and Information please contact our EU representative GPSR@taylorandfrancis.com
Taylor & Francis Verlag GmbH, Kaufingerstraße 24, 80331 München, Germany

www.ingramcontent.com/pod-product-compliance
Lightning Source LLC
Chambersburg PA
CBHW081422230426
43668CB00016B/2317